WHY NO' ...?
From Trinidad to Albert Square
via Empire Road

A Memoir

Corinne Skinner Carter
As told to Z. Nia Reynolds

Black Stock Books
Black Stock Media Ltd.

Why Not me?
From Trinidad to Albert Square *via* Empire Road
A Memoir
by Corinne Skinner Carter
As told to Z. Nia Reynolds

First published in 2011 by Black Stock Books
Black Stock Media Ltd.
©2011 Corinne Skinner Carter and Z. Nia Reynolds.

Cover design by Sarah Edwards sarsquare@hotmail.co.uk
Design by Karia Communications
Front cover photo: ©Foto Luxardo
Back cover photo: ©Corinne Skinner Carter

Printed and bound in Great Britain by MPG Biddles Ltd. King's Lynn

ISBN: 978-0-9540387-3-1

www.blackstockphotos.com
blackstockmedia@gmail.com

WHY NOT ME?
A Memoir

To Jo

All the best

Cormnd 6

Why Not Me?

Contents

Dedication:

In loving memory *of my husband, Trevor and my sister Lorna.*

*And for my children:
Dian-Marie and Michel (Courtney).*

FOREWORD

Z. Nia Reynolds

I grew up seeing Corinne Skinner Carter on television. Not in huge starring roles, but, then again, at various points, there were very few Black* performers who were given that privilege.

Over the years, in the evolution of British television, we have had episodes where we thought the times they were a-changing; with blips of progressive activity where prospects appeared to be opening up for Black performers and other professionals, only to find a reversal to an apparent default position with opportunities so few and far between as to appear non-existent.

Sometimes, 'back in the day', there would be a great deal of commotion in a household whenever a Black person appeared on screen – I mean outside the stereotypical news stories of crime and disorder. There was usually no shortage of representation in that regard.

Then, we became used to seeing Trevor McDonald reading the news at ITN, and thereafter Lenny Henry also became a bit of a fixture.

Two other faces made intermittent appearances: the late Norman Beaton and Corinne Skinner Carter, who had made BBC history with the first Black drama series, *Empire Road*.

Many years later, I had the opportunity to interview Norman Beaton and found a brilliant thinker who had insightful perceptions

---

*   In this publication, the use of the word Black (in the introduction section) is
     used affirmatively in respect of people of African heritage and diaspora, while
     maintaining the more traditional and grammatical connotation ('black') in the
     autobiographical section.

about the opportunities and limitations afforded Black performers in the UK industry.

I had heard that he was a fine dramatic actor, although I never had the opportunity to witness any of his serious or classical performances. I was used to him playing comedy, for which he was accomplished, with excellent timing.

And to think, this erudite man had appeared in a television commercial for ginger (or was it orange or coconut?) biscuits and had been given the line: "I knows it; I grows it!"

The opportunity to interview Corinne came about much later when I approached her for my documentary, *Looking for Claudia Jones*, about the civil rights activist with whom she had worked in the 1950s and 1960s. As a result of those discussions, the chance came about to work with Corinne on her memoirs.

I am fascinated by oral history and first-person accounts of a range of historical experiences. My work with the Oral History Project, and the book and exhibition, *When I Came to England (2001)*, are dedicated to capturing, for posterity, many of those reminiscences about Black life in pre- and post-war Britain.

Corinne's experiences of a life in the entertainment industry since the 1950s, when she came to this country (with the ambition of becoming a teacher), is an interesting story in itself, in which she offers many insights into what she calls her 'accidental showbiz career'.

As she explains, she did not necessarily go looking for work in the entertainment industry, but, somehow, time and again 'work found her', and, thus, a career was born. The rest is history, and that is what this book is about.

In this memoir Corinne describes growing up in colonial Trinidad and being part of a community that would gift the world with pan music and carnival; of the irresistible urge to dance, and of working with the formidable brothers, Boscoe and Geoffrey Holder; of coming to the UK to study teaching and instead becoming a performer, as she says, "in anything and everything that called for a black dancer."

As a result, the teacher training ambitions stayed on hold for many years as Corinne found herself among the post-war wave of

Black performers breaking through and finding work in television, film and the theatre during the 1950s and '60s.

Corinne's story is also very interesting from the point of view of the diverse social histories that form a backdrop to her memories, and also from the perspective of a personal history of life in the post-war British entertainment industry. It is also a valuable documentary of Black screen heritage.

Her memoir will be a welcome addition to the growing repository of oral narratives which reveal so many insights that the mainstream history books often consider marginal or irrelevant.

Commentary

Imruh Bakari

My first real contact with Corinne Skinner Carter was during the shoot of Menelik Shabazz's film, *Burning an Illusion (1981)*. This film was shot mainly in West London with a cast of young Black actors, including Cassie McFarlane, who played the lead character, Pat.

Most of the cast had either recently left drama school or had been to the Anna Scher Community Theatre in Islington, north London, which was noted for offering a good grounding in theatre and acting skills, while building on raw talent.

The cast of *Burning an Illusion* was made up of many who had had that opportunity and were now about to embark on professional careers.

Corinne Skinner Carter, who played Pat's mother, was one the few mature actors on set. Her screen presence had already been established in the BBC TV series *Empire Road (1978)*.

Along with Norman Beaton and Joe Marcell, this series had brought a new and more believable air to the representation of Black people in British entertainment television. Some might argue that the achievement of this series was partly to account for its short life on television, because, after two series, it was discontinued.

For those of us working in film, television or theatre at the time, there was a critical awareness of the limited opportunities accessible to any Black person who was pursuing a career in those areas. Because of this, *Burning an Illusion* was a rare and important event for all who were involved.

Corinne's role was relatively small: the film was about the young people, not the parents. On set, however, as a more experienced performer, her unassuming and powerful presence was always evident.

Like so many film acting performances, it is the ability to focus acquired skill and experience into a brief moment and make it memorable, which really counts. Corinne was able to do just that in the few minutes that she is on screen.

In one of these moments, Pat is at her parents' home, lounging in the sitting-room watching television when the telephone rings. Through an open door we see into the corridor where her mother is answering the phone.

Of course, we are aware that Pat's boyfriend, Del (Victor Romero Evans), is on the line. The mother makes her typical enquiries about who is calling, then moves towards the sitting-room to announce, "Pat, is one of you concubines dem."

As simple as this may sound, that brief performance says a lot about Corinne as an actor. There is an ordinariness, which could be deceptive, that very much makes her an exceptional performer.

Within the limited scope offered by British film, television and theatre there has been little opportunity to see this quality in action. This, I think, has been a reason why Corinne, in particular, is not much more highly regarded.

A glimpse of this special quality is evident in Martina Attille's *Dreaming Rivers (1987)*. Made some ten years after *Empire Road*, a lot had changed. The Black independent film movement had already made its presence felt. New ways of working had been established and new ways had been found to do work that would not necessarily be sanctioned by 'mainstream' film and television. In this context, *Dreaming Rivers* was possible.

It is a film which dramatises the intimate feelings of loss and longing as felt by an older Caribbean woman as she reflects on her life in Britain. There is not much dialogue, but the impressionist setting and the screen presence of Corinne makes this film one of the outstanding productions of 1980s British cinema, in my opinion.

In spite of that, this was not particularly a recognisable career-building moment. Black actors is Britain, in the past at least, did not have many of those moments. In a sense, this was all part of the frustration of being a professional from Africa or the Caribbean based in Britain.

Corinne was by no means a victim of these circumstances. She has always been able to maintain a highly-regarded reputation among those who know her. She always seemed to be aware of the value of what I have called her 'ordinariness'.

During the period of the making and release of *Burning an Illusion*, urban riots were raging in London's Brixton and in other British cities. In my own work, the documentary *Riots and Rumours of Riots (1981)*, was also being produced.

The film looked at the experiences of those who had lived through the Notting Hill and Nottingham riots of 1958 and the murder of Kelso Cochrane in 1959, against the backdrop of events in Britain that had culminated in the Brixton riots.

In the course of doing my research, the importance of Claudia Jones and her newspaper, the *West Indian Gazette,* could not be escaped.

Importantly, as many of my informants confirmed, Claudia Jones was not simply a political activist, but someone who gave full attention to the arts and cultural expression.

The group of people who were attracted to her were also encouraged to develop and pursue their own professional work. Among them were people like Corinne and her late husband, Trevor Carter, who was also an educator and political activist. They were also part of the Carnival movement in Britain since the beginning, and Corinne continues that connection.

This link between arts, education and political work is part of an established Caribbean tradition, and Corinne, in her quiet, dignified ordinariness, is an exemplification of this tradition.

Imruh Bakari is an actor, director and lecturer.

A personal tribute

Nina Baden-Semper

I have known Corinne for more years than I can remember. She and I have been friends since the 1960s and have been through both good times and rough.

I first met Corinne when we both danced with the Boscoe Holder Dance Company and, therefore, we were able to perform in many exciting European cities, such as Bratislavia and Prague. The audience had never seen anything like this and we were treated like royalty.

Work for Black actors and actresses in the sixties and seventies was very thin on the ground so we had to supplement our talents by doing other things.

I do remember one such time when we both bought knitting machines and started knitting and selling tights. Corinne also had a unique gift for doing crochet work and taught me how to do it, so we were able to sell goods that we had made.

Corinne's beauty lies in her having an amazing bone structure and her face reflects this. She also has truly long legs which gives her an unusual advantage of height. She is also a very talented actress and has proved this in many of the productions in which she has appeared.

Family Portrait:
Corinne (seated on bench, front left) with members of her family in a portrait taken to send to her father in the United States. Behind is her grandmother, Blanche (2nd left), and her aunt, 'Mudsy' (standing, 2nd right). Corinne's brothers are: Leslie (standing, front left), Harold (seated, centre), Courtney (seated, right); Cousins: Vilma (front, 2nd left), Myrna (2nd, right), Lucille (standing, left), Carlton (centre, back), and Barbara (standing, right).

Chapter One

Like a Motherless Child

Hold fast to dreams,
For when dreams go;
Life is a barren field,
Frozen with snow.
(Langston Hughes)[*]

My mother died when I was eight years old. I am not sure if she was a very nervous person, but I remember there was something about her always saying that she was sure she was going to die because she didn't want to be alive when there was a war going on and the world was full of turmoil.

Having lived through World War One, the war that was supposed to 'end all wars', I suppose she was anxious about military conflict and all the upheaval that accompanied it. But, not withstanding that, I was always racked with a sense of guilt that somehow I might have been responsible for her death.

The reason for my remorse was that she had become ill as a result of taking me from where we were living in Barataria, in the east of Trinidad, to visit my grandparents in Port of Spain, the capital city, for the Christmas holidays. On the way it poured with rain and we got soaking wet.

When the rain falls in Trinidad, it really falls, and this particular day we were so wet that we had to get clean clothes to put on when we arrived at my grandparents' house. Actually, I think I was all right, while she was wet through.

---

[*]   Langston Hughes, Harlem Renaissance poet (1902-1967)

I suppose she had done everything a mother would do to make sure I was protected but she was completely soaked. She left me in Port of Spain and returned home but subsequently became ill with pneumonia. Within 21 days, she was dead.

For such a long time I carried a sense of guilt that if my mother hadn't taken me to my grandparents and got wet on the way, she wouldn't have got sick and died.

As it turns out, she expired nine months after my uncle Tony, her brother, who died from electric shock. He was an electrician and went to work one day to fix some damaged wire on a telegraph pole but got electrocuted and fell off the structure.

They picked him up and took him to the rum shop and revived him there before taking him home, but he didn't quite recover. I think my great aunt called everyone out and so the elders were with him when he died three days later, on an Easter Monday.

The next day they had a post-mortem, which, in those days, they always did at the house. So, they moved him into the dining room or the drawing room (which was like the lounge) and I heard the people saying that when they opened him up they didn't see any blood. Apparently there was nothing to scrub up when they did the autopsy, no doubt because rigor mortis had set in, but it intrigued me for years that 'Uncle Tony had no blood'.

And I saw that they had stitched him up after the examination. The stitching was done with thick crochet cotton or wool, like the kind they use to stitch those heavy French jumpers, and it came right up to his neck. That was quite scary to see. My uncle was alive and walking around one day, then stitched up like that the next.

Now, an incident like the sudden death of a relative would be a tragedy for most people but for us children it wasn't really such a catastrophe because of the way in which we'd been brought up. The adults had raised us in such a way that we would not make too much of a commotion about it.

My parents were so Victorian that they didn't make a fuss over things like that for us to see. It was always that stiff upper lip that was associated with the upper-classes in England. I can't remember anybody at any funeral ever bawling. And, I can't remember anybody in our family crying, for that matter.

Crying in public would have been so embarrassing, as far as they were concerned. It was just not the done thing to make a fuss or to get openly emotional. Even when there was a death in the family.

When somebody wasn't there, they just weren't there and somebody else would have to do what that person used to do; life goes on. At least they didn't make a fuss for us children to know that something was wrong.

A bereavement affected them in their way and, of course, they must have grieved, but we never saw all that. We were quite safe and comfortable and that was OK.

In the West Indies in those days when I was a child, during the 1930s, if you died one day they would bury you the next; they didn't keep the body any longer than two days. So, the day after Uncle Tony's death they had to get up early and go out to collect flowers to make the wreathes before the burial.

It was more or less the same with my mother. When she first got sick I don't think anyone actually thought it would be fatal. In those days they used to say that if you got pneumonia and you lived to see seven days they would say you were doing all right and they would give you up to fourteen days. Well, she got the seven and the fourteen but she died within the 21 days.

I have this vivid memory of my brother, Mervyn, who was two years younger than me, going around telling everybody that his head was burning up because his mother had died.

The poor thing clamped his hands on his head and kept saying, 'Me head hot, me head hot!'

Perhaps he was saying that his head was hurting.

I can't remember much about the actual funeral. In those days, all funerals left from the house of the person who had died, they didn't take it to a mortuary or anything like that.

What I do remember is that before the service, when the coffin was still at the house, some people picked up my brother and I and 'crossed us over' the coffin. That is to say, we were lifted high in the air by a pair of strong arms and passed over the coffin to another set of waiting hands while the people sang and said nice, reassuring things to us. That is all part of the old-time culture and apparently was supposed to stop us having bad dreams about our dead mother.

I vaguely remember some of the hymns that they sang at the house: Abide *with Me, It is Well with my Soul*, songs like that, but I can't recall the funeral procession or even going to the cemetery. I knew where she was buried but I don't think that realisation came at the funeral; I think it came some time afterwards.

When I was growing up there was a great sense of fear about death and I think that was the reason for them crossing us over the coffin. That act, which some people will call superstitious, was supposed to help us forget the awfulness of what had happened. So that if we did remember we would do so in a nice way because, in those days, whenever somebody died you were scared to go into the room where the person had been.

In fact, you were petrified to go anywhere that the person had gone when they were alive. And, because most people usually died in the house where they lived, you wouldn't want to go to bed at night unless someone else was there with you.

Fortunately for me, our family never slept in darkness; the house was always full of light and up to this day, at my mature age, I still do not sleep in the dark. I simply cannot sleep in the dark. If there is no light on, I cannot sleep; I feel as though I am being stifled. I can't handle darkness.

If I go to hotels and am there alone I have to leave the television on all night for company and to light up the room. I don't need a bright light, but there must be some form of illumination. And I must be able to see my hand in front of my face because of the fear that 'The booboo man will come to get me', as we used to say as children.

In the old days if you were naughty they would tell you that a 'booboo man' was going to get you if you didn't behave. They would never have told you that the 'jumbie man' was going to get you because that was too extreme; too evil.

Jumbie was a ritual thing and that was a lot worse than a booboo man, which was moderately frightening in comparison. A jumbie man, now, was something else entirely. It was a demonic entity connected with voodoo, sacrifices and fearsome things like that.

That's why we were scared of Mother Moore, the Shango Woman, who lived opposite us. We feared her because she might have had a jumbie there at her house where she held her mysterious Shango-Baptist religious meetings.

We weren't exposed to a lot of fear as children. We had a very loving family. My mother's name was Iris (*nee* Griffin) and she was quite a lot younger than my father, Harold Skinner, when they married. He later travelled and went to live in the United States.

My grandmother used to sing songs in patois. She spoke a lot of patois, the French dialect from Martinique, where she came from. Most of her extended family spoke the language and a lot of them couldn't or wouldn't speak English.

We never did learn to speak patois, though. That was a deliberate decision not to let us children learn the language because they wanted us to speak English. They were very colonial-minded. They used to say that the slave owners had taken away the language of the slaves because they wanted them to speak English and if they didn't they couldn't go to school and get an education.

My mother never spoke the patois, none of my grandmother's children did, and granny was a cunning old bird who used to speak patois when she didn't want them to know what she was saying.

In turn, my mother learned to speak a dialect they called 'gibberish' and she used to speak that when she wanted to tell other people something that she didn't want us to understand. So there were all these secret languages going on and as children we were completely mystified by them.

My grandmother on my mother's side was named Justine but we called her 'Ma', and my aunts all had French names like Tantie Atille, Tantie Ernestine, Tantie Yontine, Tantie Rose, and Tantie Elouise. They dressed in these long clothes and billowing skirts with acres of petticoats underneath.

Tantie Atille always had her head tied but my grandmother's head wasn't tied, so you could see a marvellous head of long, silver-coloured hair that was her crowning glory.

She often wore two long plaits that were thick as two plantains, but she had a problem with her hair because people always wanted to comb it and she hated people fussing over her hair.

I think I took that from her because I also hate people poking around with the top of my head. I started combing my own hair when I was about nine because I just could not stand anybody pulling my hair when they were combing it.

For years I did not go to the hairdresser's because I cannot abide people toying with or playing with my hair; it is a no-go zone for me. I can't take the tugging and the fussing, the way some people pull your hair. It's only about two years or so ago that I started going to the hairdresser's, but that's usually for something very simple. Most of the time, I do my hair myself.

This particular grandmother, Justine, was a strong old lady and very elegant. She always wore skirts with flouncy blouses and these graceful, lacy petticoats underneath the skirts. You would never find her dressed without her petticoats. Even in the house she would be formally dressed every single day.

I don't know how those old people used to dress like that because it was so hot! We used to call her tops 'chemise' and she would wear her blouse on top of the chemise and sometimes the blouse would be worn over the top of the skirt.

She used to tell us stories about how the French people behaved in Martinique and everything about her was dignified and formal, almost regal.

We were very middle class and we were always aware of our place and class and there were codes of conduct, categories of people we would have associated with and others we were told to avoid.

There was a cardinal rule: we were forbidden from eating on the street. That was a definite no-no and if anybody saw us doing that and told on us, we would get licks. Whatever I had to eat, even if it was a fruit or some candy, I'd have to bring it home and eat it there.

I called my great aunt Tante Tante and that's the French creole for 'great aunt'. In those days we called our real aunts, that is our aunts who were blood relatives, 'tante' or 'tantie', and the respectful way of addressing older, unrelated women was to call them 'auntie'.

So, you would have Tantie Elouise and Tantie this or that, but if I said, 'Auntie Evelyn', that was no relation but a polite salutation, instead of saying Mrs Evelyn or Mrs Jordan. Likewise, men were all addressed as 'uncle'.

I used to call my mother, 'Mammie', but a lot of people in our community who didn't have the French influence used to call their mothers 'Mum' or 'Mother', but mostly 'Mother'.

My grandmother on my father's side was named Blanche, and we called her 'Granny'. She was half-African and half-Scottish and she was a tall, slim, very proud-looking lady with strikingly beautiful hazel-coloured eyes which my father and, subsequently, my daughter inherited.

When we were children, we didn't have a wireless to start with so we made our own entertainment. Growing up, we used to have our musical evenings and those went on right up to the time when my uncle and my mother died.

Afterwards, things changed, but only in the sense that those members of the family were no longer there and were sorely missed. But we would still have little concerts among ourselves and we children would get up and sing, recite a poem or organise entertainment that involved the whole family. Our close friends would come and join in.

I can remember performing as a three-year-old in one of our family concerts that we sometimes held in the evenings. It was at Christmas time and I would have been four the following March. That was my first ever 'public performance'.

I can't remember exactly what I did, but I remember getting up on the 'stage' that they made and singing and dancing with the family as a group and then performing by myself.

Around that time I was going to a private nursery school, and I suppose whatever we were doing there had given me a measure of confidence and some material for my performance. Everyone was apparently regaled by the show I put on, and, of course, I was feted and made a fuss of. And to think that later on when I started dancing for a living my grandmother did not like it at all. In fact, she strongly objected and she used to say, "Nice young ladies don't dance or get on the stage."

She never came to see me perform, ever, and she kept the same stance all her life. But it wasn't just that she didn't come to see me, she didn't go anywhere anyway, unless it was to church.

Before my mother died, when I was about six or seven, I decided I was going to do my first communion. I got caught up in all the preparations at church without my family knowing anything about it. I took my instructions over a number of weeks and passed the test, or whatever it was that enabled me to take communion.

I went home on the day before the ceremony and told my grandmother and Mammie that they were to get me a white dress and a veil for my first communion. After the initial shock, they went crazy. They couldn't believe what they were hearing and asked me who told me to do that and I said, "But everybody else was taking lessons so I went and took the lessons too."

What could they do? They couldn't do anything about it because it was too late. They chastised me by saying I should have told them and they would have made sure I did it properly rather than me taking it upon myself to do these things. I wasn't even big enough to come from school by myself but yet I had found the courage to do that. They must have thought I was downright rude and 'boldface' rather than thinking I was showing initiative at such a young age.

All I could think about was dressing up and looking resplendent in a white dress and veil with all the pomp and ceremony. Besides, it looked like fun!

I did feel privileged as a child. Up to this day I always say that I have never thought of myself as being unlucky. No matter what has happened to me, somebody has had it worse than me.

Even as a child I was always aware of being lucky and my grandmother always used to tell me that I was fortunate, so I took her word for it. She used to say, "This is one lucky child!"

I didn't always feel lucky, though. During Mother's Day you always had to wear a white poppy if your mother was dead and a red poppy if she was alive. So, I had to wear a white poppy from an early age, but I never felt unwanted because of that.

As a matter of fact, I used to feel that I had a lot more given to me because I didn't have a mother and my father was so far away in America. So, I was unlucky in one way but there were compensations in so many other ways.

The first time in my life when I felt that I was missing something was when I was much older and I saw a friend called Jean Belgrave sitting in her mother's lap and I don't know why that made me feel forlorn because I always had two grandmothers' laps to sit on and Jean didn't even have one grandmother because they were both dead. But, at that precise moment, I felt terribly sad that my mother wasn't alive.

I am not a very emotional person. My parents weren't emotional so I don't think I missed anything as far as that was concerned. I never really experienced their loss in the sense of feeling emotional about it. But that incident, seeing Jean so close to her mother, really struck me and I'll never forget it. It became stuck in my memory and I don't know why. Yet, the way my grandparents treated me they probably over-compensated for the loss of my mother, so I never felt like a motherless child.

Now I think about it, they probably went out of their way to make sure that I never had to say, "If I had a mother I would have done X, Y and Z."

The fact that I lost my mother at a young age was not so harrowing because I was well-protected by my grandmothers and my aunts. In that sense, I had many surrogate 'mothers' caring for me.

Yes, my grandparents really did take care of me as a child. And I'm sure my mother couldn't have helped me any more than I have been helped throughout my life. I got my education, I got my scholarship to go to secondary school, and I got a career in the entertainment industry with a few awards – although I could always do with some more.

Chapter Two

Chatterbox

What made me really happy as a child? As long as I could have a group of people to play with and talk with, then I was just as happy as I could be. I *loved* to talk.

When I went to school I was among the most popular ones; I was never on the sidelines. I used to get involved in all sorts of activities; whatever was going on, there I was right in the thick of things.

As a child there were all the usual rituals of the carefree and innocent years: climbing trees, running, jumping, pitching marbles, flying kites and out-performing the boys. I was very outward and a bit of a tomboy.

With a sigh of exasperation, the grown-ups always used to say "Corinne take a rest, please."

I couldn't be precocious, though, because my grandmother was very Victorian and if you even frowned she would ask you, "Who do you think you are?"
You wouldn't dare scowl in front of her.

But there was nothing I enjoyed more than a good chat. If anybody came along I would fill them up with talk. And not only that, I never had friends my own age; they were always older than me.

I mean, when I was a child of about ten-years-old one of my friends had a daughter that was older than me. I never got to know the daughter, although her mother introduced me to her. I was friends with the mother, not the girl who was closer to my age.

And again, Ione Joslyn was a person who was old enough to be working while I was still going to school, but she was my friend.

My friends were never children my age, and the age difference was never just a few years, either. It was always something like this: I was in the first grade and they were in the fifth grade, working or even married with children of their own.

My grandmother used to say, "You like big people's company", in a very disapproving, judgmental way, but it didn't faze me.

I still used to do what children did, like pitching marbles, but when it came to talking, I used to fill up the older people's ears with gossip and, like me, they were always very incorrigible when it came to chatting about other people's business.

And I was always so independent. When I was about nine, and considered big enough to go to Sunday school on my own, I remember that one time after service my brother and I decided to go for a walk. You know, on Sunday evenings, people always went for afternoon walks and we children welcomed any opportunity to stray.

On this particular occasion, we had so much time to kill and everything was so peaceful and free. I decided to take my brother to a place called The Mang (short for mangrove), which was at the back of Barataria.

It was quite remote, full of canefields and was quite swampy. There weren't any houses there then (although there are houses there now). And it was a group of us who went, including Erma Hellier (who later married the publisher John la Rose). As children she was my very good friend and neighbour.

The area (The Mang) was out of bounds to us, but I took it upon myself to follow the group. My grandmother would always say that I used to drift or daydream.

When we got back home our shoes were muddy and they asked us where we had been. I told them "We went to The Mang".
I got licks for that and never went back there again.

During the week the routine was that we used to get up in the morning and, before school, we had tea. At lunch time we had our breakfast, which was the main meal of the day and we would go home for that.

For the main meal we would have food like chicken, rice, potatoes, plantain, cassava: good, home-cooked food and then we'd go back to school.

There was a place called The Breakfast Shed that used to deliver food to the schools, but we didn't have that meal, we went home for our breakfast. Then, when school was over and we got home, we had 'lunch', which was a snack and, at about six o'clock, we had our 'tea', which was high tea with sandwiches followed by cake, ice-cream or something equally scrumptious.

At my grandmother's house during the holidays, every day after we had lunch we had to wash our hands and go and sleep. I hated that. I couldn't stand the idea of sleeping during the day and my other grandmother agreed with me. She didn't like the idea of sleeping in the day because she thought it was a sign of laziness.

We didn't have electric light then, we had those lovely old oil lamps around the house. You used to put in the pitch oil and turn the wick and that would give a beautiful, bright light.

We also had a chandelier. I think that was my grandmother's French influence from Martinique. In those days we also had a coal pot, which we would fill up with coal and put the irons in there to heat up to press the clothes. Long afterwards we got a wireless and things like that.

Those were the nice days, yes! Although, to be honest, I didn't think of them as nice days at the time.

Nowadays, you see people running out to buy these old things because it's nostalgic. People pay a fortune for them at the antique shops. When we were younger we couldn't wait to get rid of that old stuff and become 'modern'.

Apart from the talking, I used to read a lot when I was a child. I was always reading story books and my imagination would run away with me. Such is the stuff of childhood.

My favourites were the Enid Blyton stories and a book of West Indian folk tales. I also loved poetry and we would learn poems by heart, which was always something to be proud of.

I cannot read as fast now as I could when I was younger, but I still love reading, even though it takes ages to finish a book. My concentration seems to go very quickly and there are lots of distractions around, but I must admit there is a bit of laziness as well.

As I said, I started going to a private school when I was very small and when I was five or six I left to go to the public 'big school', and was in the infants. There were three stages in the infants and the third stage was called the 'introductory stage', which was the phase before you went to the next 'big school': the juniors, when you were aged 7 or 8.

In junior school I took part in everything. I was very competitive and had to win all my races. I couldn't bear to lose.

In primary school we wore pinafores: 'pinnies', with ribbons in our hair and by secondary school it was blouse and skirt, while the boys blue shirts and short khaki pants.

And, of course, in those days, we would line up in the yard at the start of the school day and the teachers would pass around and inspect our nails, hair, behind our ears, and check if our shoes were polished. If we were slovenly we would get hit with a ruler or they would call our parents to come to school and explain why their child was coming to school in that condition.

Schools were very strict; very Victorian. We had respect for people and children knew their place. If I did something wrong and got smacked for it I didn't dare go home and say I got spanked. The first thing my grandmother would have asked was, "What did you do?"

To her, I must have done something or the teacher would not have chastised me, so I would have got another beating on top of the one I got at school. We learned discipline in school and at home our parents ruled us with their eyes. We would know we were in trouble just by the expression on their faces, so we learned to behave.

If we were late for school or we'd been naughty and thought we were going to be disciplined, we'd get three stones and throw them behind us with a prayer that there wouldn't be a beating and then walk straight ahead with our heads held high, no looking back. That was the way to ward off punishment, especially licks. Most of the time it worked, or at least we convinced ourselves that it did.

In truth, maybe they didn't want to beat us that day, but we just thought our spell had worked.

After morning inspection we had assembly and then we would begin lessons. We had slates in the primary school then books in the older school, with pencils and pens with an inkwell on the desk. And we had the times tables on the back of the exercise books, so we would have to learn them by rote and the whole class would sing-song: 'one-times-two-is-two, two-times-two-are-four...' and so on.

We also had something called 'mental' where the teacher would stand in the front and call out some sums and we had to write the answer.

He or she would say, "OK, five times six is?" and point to someone. You had to know it. And we had dictation where he would call out a whole sentence and we had to write it down. When you were little, dictation was only a sentence but as we got older it was a whole passage.

If you ever went into a classroom at any time there would be complete silence and if we were making noise all that the teacher had to do was tap on the desk with his ruler and say, 'Fingers on your lips!'

Everyone would stop talking and we would sit there with our fingers on our lips until the teacher said we could move. Anyone who was naughty would be called out and made to kneel down in front of the class until teacher said you could get up. It was either that or standing in a corner until you were allowed to go. It was a shameful thing having to face that corner with everybody looking at you.

I never had to kneel down but I did get licks with the strap once for talking and once was enough. I learned my lesson and was determined I wasn't going to get beaten a second time.

I didn't stop chatting, though. Instead, I learned to be very clever about talking so that I would never be caught, and I wasn't. There's a real knack to that: you posture yourself quietly as though you're paying attention and whisper whatever you have to say as though you were a ventriloquist. I could keep that up for ages – and I did.

Why Not Me?

It's ironic that I was such a chatterbox because I used to stammer as a child. I stammered a lot and I still do sometimes, which is why I hate making speeches or giving presentations. The thought of that makes me break out in a cold sweat and you are likely to hear my knees knocking.

If I have a script or I've learned my lines, then it's a lot less daunting, but don't expect me to extemporise because I become a nervous wreck and the main fear is that the stammering will come on in front of a crowd of people. I don't want to make a fool of myself so I don't make speeches off the cuff. If I have a script or a prompt, then I'm fine.

When I was a child my aunt used to shout at me for stammering and when she shouted, all the words would fly out. I just used to blurt out whatever I was trying to say. It was quite unpleasant. It became a lot better as I went into adulthood, but sometimes, even now, the stammering still happens. The doctor says that my brain goes faster than my tongue and that's what causes the problem.

The problem didn't really affect my learning because when I went to the 'big school' I was moved up a year or two because I was ahead of the other children.

The private school that I'd attended had used a teaching series called Royal Readers, a set of old English books that were used in England at the same time and were more advanced than the silly books they were using for children in our local schools.

My sophisticated seven-year-old self found those books to be very babyish. By the time I got to the big school I skipped two grades. At that time reading meant a lot, although my maths did not come on as good as the reading because they always prioritised reading over numeracy.

As children we played a lot; it was wonderful. We had kite fights and bike races with my cousins and we used to make stilts and climb up on top of the kitchen and get on them and walk around like giants. Those types of stilts were like the ones the old time people used for their parades, which we called Moko Jumbie. It was a festival that paid homage to the spirits.

In those days when you visited relatives you spent the whole day. On one occasion I was with my cousin David and the rest of the children playing with a pair of roller skates.

We were taking it in turn to skate to the corner and turn back. When it was my turn, I had just set off when someone called out from the house, "Come home, it's time for tea", and I shouted out, "One more skate."

I skated down to the corner by the lamppost, fell straight down and landed on my hand. I thought straight away that it was broken.

They got me up and took me to the house and as we got there I cried out to David's grandmother, "Tantie Lily, Tantie Lily, look, I broke my hand."

She said to me, "Don't be so stupid, come and have your tea."

So I had the tea and then went home to my house and told my Aunt Mudsy, "I broke my hand you know, but Tantie Lily didn't take any notice of me."

And she said, 'Corinne, everything is excitement for you. Why must you always exaggerate?'

She wasn't convinced either but to pacify me she added "Go by Mr Protine and let him give you something for it."

Mr Protine was the chemist. I went to him and he gave me some 'sugar-of-lead', which was like granules or a powder that you mixed with water and applied to the where the pain was on your body.

Afterwards, he bandaged my hand and sent me back home. Sugar-of-lead works for sprains and bruises but wouldn't work for a broken hand!

The next morning my grandmother arrived and I told her, "Granny, I told them I broke my hand but nobody's taking any notice of me. Look at it!"

By this time my hand was very swollen and I could hardly move it. My grandmother (my father's mother) went crazy. She was furious and said, "The child told you all she broke she hand and you didn't pay her any notice!"

They must have thought I was telling stories like the boy who cried wolf. They always used to dismiss me and say, "Here she goes again; so excitable."

They couldn't even get my blouse on; they had to cut the sleeve to get my hand through it. As soon as I was dressed my grandmother took me on the tram car to the hospital and it turned out that the hand was broken in two places and they had to manipulate it to reset it and put it in a splint. Well, the splint was another thing for me to show off about!

That happened when I was about nine and I was off school for about six weeks, although it was the left hand that was broken and I could still have written with my right.

I used to climb up on the concrete wall at the back of our house and look over into the school, so I knew when it was play time. I used to wave to the children and they would all clamber to the window to see me waving to them.

I must have enjoyed being off school, but at the same time I was a bit bored and envious of the children who were in school. I had nothing better to do than to go and climb up and draw attention to myself although I had to do lots of reading and sums because Auntie wouldn't let me get away with doing nothing.

Still, whenever I had my chance and she was out of the way, I would climb up on the wall and regale my schoolmates – even a broken hand didn't stop me.

On Sunday evenings we would go up to The Pitch, a paved area around the savannah, which is three and a half miles round. Nowadays, they say it's the world's biggest roundabout because they use it as a roundabout, except at carnival time. There are all these benches on the Pitch and everyone would go up there with their parents and friends to promenade.

At a certain point in this area there is a dip which we called the Hollow and on the brightest moonlit night of the month they had a band concert in there and people used to come from all over to attend that event.

Everybody would know when the concert was going to be and we children would go with our parents. It used to be the classical bands: the police band, the orphanage band, and the regiment band, not just any old band, just the top ones and it was all classical music then.

There would be so much excitement: "Are you to going band concert tonight?" The word would spread like wildfire. We grew up with those classical concerts and it was thrilling.

Depending on where they lived from the Pitch, people's parents would go up there for their early morning walk from about four o'clock, buy their bananas or other fruits, and go back home, have their breakfast and go off to work.

It was like a ritual. Those older people had friends that they would meet at The Pitch and they used to go in the mornings and pass some time socialising, getting their morning exercise. They continued with this until they were up in age, even into their nineties.

Our side of the Pitch had a big clock which chimed like Big Ben, the famous English clock, so everybody could hear it and we'd go up there and the clock would chime and let us know when it was time for them to go back home.

When we were children, the adults always used to say to us, 'Don't let six o'clock catch you out of doors, you know.'

And we couldn't give any excuses because the clock would chime and we would hear it and so would they. If we came in late, we'd get licks.

We were allowed to spend time with each other as children, and our parents knew and approved of our friends.

At school there were a few children that I wasn't supposed to mix with and my grandmother called them 'The rab'.

She'd say, "I don't want to see you with that little rab, you know."

I think it comes from Arab, used in a derogatory way, or it might have been rabble, but knowing how things were in those days I feel it was the former. They always called naughty people 'rabs, scamps and scallywags'.

I maintained the friendships from my school days throughout my life, and some of those school friends even became my children's godparents. For example, as I mentioned, I've known Erma La Rose since I was six or seven years old.

In our little group we had about three boys and one of them was very effeminate. We called him 'Girly George' but we didn't mean it in a malicious way; he was our best friend. We didn't know anything about homosexuality then, but he grew up to be gay. Nowadays, people are more knowledgeable and understanding of these things.

In the old days our friends became closer in a way because we needed to invent our fun rather than relying on computers like they do today.

We played hopscotch, a ball game called 'love-in', dodging was a team game, so were rounders and a game called 'bean bag'. We made and flew kites and made and spun gigs. And we used to have kite fights, which were very competitive.

Interestingly, when I lived in Woodbrook we were literally just around the corner from where I went to school. That's how I was able to climb up and wave to the children when I was off school with a broken hand.

We lived in the second house on the bend at number 1 Picton Street and the school was on Tragarite Road, which, incidentally, was about three doors down from where a certain school mate of mine lived. His name was Trevor Carter.

Chapter Three

Mudsy

We called my aunt 'Mudsy' because her last daughter, my cousin Myrna, couldn't say mother: she used to say 'Mudsy', so the name just stuck on. Everyone in the area called her that, except her first three children who always called her 'Mother'.

Mudsy's proper name was Mildred Henry and she was my father's sister and one of the people who more or less adopted me after my mother died. I was raised with her children not as though we were cousins but as if we were all siblings.

Interestingly, Mudsy and I looked so alike that no-one knew that she was my aunt and not my birth mother. Saying that, I also resembled her children: Lucille, Barbara and Carlton to such an extent that no one outside the family would have known that we weren't brothers and sisters by blood.

Mudsy was a warm, friendly, very maternal woman and a wonderful cook. She would never do anything rash or administer discipline when she was in a temper. If we had misbehaved, she would always sleep on it and then decide our fate, sometimes a day or so later.

Back in those days some people reared animals like goats and cows, and almost everyone had chickens and ducks in their yard. Mudsy always had a lot of poultry and we children had our own pet chicken or duck.

We'd adopt a particular yard bird and say, "Blanket is mine". The eggs it laid were shared by everybody at home and the owner of the productive pet would go to school with an extra spring in their step and proudly announce, "Do you know my fowl is laying eggs. She laid four overnight and we had them for breakfast!"

There weren't many high spirits when Mudsy decided to treat us to fried chicken for dinner, however.

The thing is we would know when they were going to slaughter a chicken or duck and that used to cause a lot of trouble, especially if it was our pet that was facing the chop. When that happened you wouldn't eat a thing because it was so hurtful to lose your 'friend', not through old age or accident but to the cooking pot. We would get sad, pout, sulk and lose our appetite for a day or two.

One Easter, there was a scarcity of chickens in the market so we didn't have chickens and got lots of pigeons instead. One day, Mudsy decided to cook pigeon for dinner. She told us that we were going to need about four or five of them and we decided to help her kill the birds.

She told us to hold the pigeon by the neck and swing it round and then drop it on the ground and that would kill it. We caught a couple and tried it, and the poor things fluttered and fluttered and then died. It was fun doing the swinging but when we saw them fluttering and lying there, dead, we felt terrible. Not one of us children ate a mouthful. My aunt ate pigeon by herself for about four days because we wouldn't touch it.

In those days, we always had sports days and fairs, especially at Christmas time. We would pay six pence to go in, during those days of pounds, shillings and pence. And, at other times, there were also lots of outings.

As a child we went to the countryside but never to the seaside. I think parents thought the seaside was too dangerous because they worried about children drowning.

Most of our outings were educational, so we would do lessons about the Pitch Lake in the south of Trinidad, which is the only resource of its kind in the world. We also went on a plantation and learned about cocoa trees, and other domestic crops, or we went hiking. Those trips were a lot of fun.

In my first year at big school my teacher was Iris Semper and we called her 'Manhead Semper', which wasn't very nice. She was the aunt of Nina Baden-Semper, who years later became famous in England in the TV show *Love thy Neighbour*.

Miss Semper, like all the teachers, was very good but very serious. There was also one called Miss Best. All the children used to be scared of her, but the parents loved her. She was buxom and she always had a whip and she would growl and control us school children like a sergeant major.

I liked a teacher called Miss Henry. She lived behind us and her mother ran a teacher training school. She was very musical and was our pianist at school and started teaching me to play the piano but I didn't keep it up. She would have some of us over to her place to sing as a group, and that was good.

Primary school children, aged around 10 or 11, had to take an exam and if they passed that they would go to either the Queen's Royal College: QRC, which was the Anglican high school, or St Mary's College. It was similar to when they had the grammar school system in England and was based on the same principles.

The brightest children when on to the top schools, and the rest, who at that time were in the fourth standard, continued in the same school.

However, there was a teacher called Mr Moore who thought that there should be a place for children who did not pass the exam but were bright enough to continue with a secondary education. He set up the J. Edgar Moore Modern Secondary School because he was socialist-minded, and he recruited teachers from different places. I think he coined the term 'secondary education' before they had that concept in England. This was in the 1940s.

The teachers were very professional and very left-wing, and, because they were like that, they knew all the children individually. If you went to QRC, St Mary's or Bishop's, which were the elite schools, you were one in a number, but in our school the teachers knew everybody and knew our parents.

We had to be really well behaved and get into our work at school, and we also had to remember that our parents depended on us to be disciplined and do well. We were almost like the colleges. Our school started at 9am and there was no interval until lunch time then we finished at four. We really had no playtime.

Mr Moore, the headmaster, was the Latin teacher and Mr Braithwaite, the deputy head, taught French. Then they got Mr

Vesprey, a maths teacher from Bishop's Boys and Mr Hayes, a geography teacher, came from somewhere else.

When that school first opened all the classes were held in one big area called Brooklyn Hall in a building which had been used by the Freemasons to hold Lodge meetings. You had a class here, a class there; about four all together. And the seniors were in one big class over on one side of the hall.

They based that school on the college system, so we had French, Latin, Spanish, all the subjects that they did in the colleges and big schools that we didn't do in the junior school.

Mr Moore also had an after school class called economics and civics (which we pronounced 'kiviks'), but only the boys went to that class, and Trevor Carter was one of them.

Interestingly enough, three of those boys actually went into politics after they left school, serving in government and that sort of thing.

We had a certain amount of children going to Modern Secondary for free, while some were full price and some paid half price. Those who had failed their exams still had a second chance to go to a better school.

Trevor paid the full fee to go to school while I paid half-fee because I had passed half the exams. Trevor always used to say, "You were brighter than me in school, you know."

The headmaster was also the type of person that if children couldn't pay their fees he would just go to the parents and have a discussion about it and he would work something out. He was a real socialist. So, Trevor became involved in his school and was a great admirer of Mr Moore. By the time he went to England he was already quite committed to the socialist cause.

Trevor and I weren't childhood sweethearts, although we grew up in the same area and even went to the same secondary school. There was no spark from my point of view. In fact, he was never in the picture when we were children. He later said that he secretly liked me from the time that I came to school but he was never on my mind or even in my eye-line.

According to Trevor, on my first day at the school someone fired a slingshot and a stone hit me in the back of my head and I turned around and slapped Trevor because I thought it was him. I later found out it was a boy called Arthur Goddard.

Unfortunately, Trevor was close enough to feel the full force of my displeasure, although he protested: "But I didn't even do it."

It was odd that I appeared to have a dislike for this young man because he was really harmless. Not that I noticed him really. And, interestingly, his aunt Gwennie and my aunt Mudsy were best friends.

There was another time when I went to Trevor's house to complain about him to his mother because I used to wear a hat to school and someone threw it up in the tree and I couldn't reach it. I marched round to Trevor's house and protested and he got told off.

I wasn't sure if it was him who had done it, but he was the nearest person to the school so he got blamed. I was very bold as a child and I am much shyer and more of a scaredy-cat now.

One day at secondary school my cousin and I went home for lunch. When we got there the lunch wasn't ready and by the time it was finished and we had eaten and gone back, it was very late and lessons had started.

As we walked up the stairs Mr Moore shouted out from one end of the hall, "Skinner and Carr get back to where you came from!" So, we made an about turn, got back on our bikes and went home. When we got there auntie said to us, "What are you doing here now?"

So we said, "Mr Moore told us to go back where we came from, so we've come back home."

She said, "That man sent you back home because my food was late!'

And she was so angry and went on and on and said, "OK, me and him tomorrow morning. I'm going to go down there and fix him!"

That evening, the headmaster turned up at our house. As he reached the gate Mudsy started, "You sent my children home because my food was late? You could have asked questions to find out what happened…"

And she went on and on at him.

He was flabbergasted. He couldn't have a go at our aunt so he had a go at us and said, "I have never come across two more cantankerous children as these. You knew very well that I didn't mean for you to go all the way back home. I thought you were fooling about in the playground and turned up late for class."

It was he who got into trouble instead of us. It was so funny. That just shows what sort of person I was at school, I was really naughty, and my cousin Jean was my partner-in-crime.

We had a big tamarind tree in the yard and my uncle was the chief superintendent for the young offenders' institute which occupied a lot of land way down in the back behind all the houses. He used to live in a huge house near the road and some of the boys from the institute used to be on duty at the house, cleaning and taking care of the place.

They used to pick our fruit for us and they would get the tamarinds and Jean and I would shell the tamarinds, put them in a jam jar, season them with salt and pepper and take the jar to school with us. Everyone wanted to have a sample of this treat. Not only that, but we used to roll the bottle from one class to another when the teachers weren't looking.

In those days, we didn't think about money, so we didn't sell them. Instead, we had fun rolling the jar on the floor and letting the other classes sample our snack. But Jean got caught one day and her punishment was to stand on the stage with the jar in her hand. She went on that stage with a lot of tamarinds in the bottle but by the time she left the stage the jar was completely empty.

Those were my 'miserable' days in school. We used to get into a lot of scrapes. When I wasn't doing athletics and playing netball or distance running and sprinting, then I was either being naughty or singing in the choir.

Sports day: I was there. Concerts: I'm there. School work, cricket, choir singing, you name it: I'm there. I always had an outgoing, competitive spirit and I had no time for boys except as rivals to be competed with or made fun of.

The worse thing we used to do was to interfere with people if we knew they had a nickname. There was a woman we called

'Britain' because she dressed up in red, white and blue and talked about the King all the time.

Another one we used to call 'Johnny Walker' because he used to walk with a cutlass, and another one we called 'Mad Elsie', and yet another one we called 'Mosquito'. Every time we passed him we used to swat ourselves as though swatting mosquitoes, and then we'd burst out laughing.

There was also a boy we used to call 'Tadpole' because he was much blacker than us. If we were 14-years-old, Tadpole would have been about 18 or 19. He was neither old nor stupid, just a young man going about his business but we decided to call him that nickname every time we saw him.

One time he tried to talk to Joyce, Jean's sister, and we 'traced him' for being so boldface in trying to chat up Joyce.

One day, we were walking to school and we saw Tadpole standing up by someone's house talking to a lady, so we started to laugh at him and as we passed we started teasing him. Well, he decided to run after us.

Not only was he older than us but the man was a cricketer and he could run! So we ran up to the end of the savannah and we didn't know where to go so we ran back down to where the Rediffusion building was and as we came to the tennis courts nearby we saw the caretaker and as we got into the place we sat on the floor without saying a word.

She said to us, "What are you doing here?"

We told her, "We came to visit."

And she said, "What is wrong?"

So we had to tell her what happened and the guy was standing up outside but he didn't dare come in. We were petrified because we had no idea what he would do if he got hold of us. The caretaker let us slip out through the back and we managed to escape but Tadpoe was still standing up outside the front waiting for us to come out.

What were we doing troubling that fellow? He was a big man to us, and I don't think we ever interfered with him again after that day. In fact, we never went anywhere near him. If we saw him we went off in a different direction. That was the end of that. But we always used to get into trouble like that.

One time Jean went and interfered with Mad Elsie and Mad Elsie hit her with a stick and when we went home we didn't dare tell our auntie about it, otherwise we would have been in a lot of trouble and would probably have been given another pummeling.

There was another man we called 'Doggie' and he came talking to us one day and we ran him, 'Go away with your dog face!'

But that backfired on me because when I went to England, he was up there. And do you know he became my good friend but he never mentioned anything about us teasing him and calling him 'Doggie' so I didn't mention it, although I felt guilty.

Merle, the aunt of my cousin David, started teaching in school after she finished her exams, just like quite a few others who had graduated from the school.

One day when Merle was teaching in a classroom the others went to go home but she never moved from the desk. She appeared to have collapsed, so they called her parents and they came to take her home. It was then that they discovered that she was dead. Up to now I do not know what happened to Merle. I was about 13 or 14 then and she would have been about 18.

It wasn't a stroke but I have a feeling that it had something to do with sickle cell as it is that side of my family that has sickle cell, although someone else thinks it might have been to do with her thyroid. But it was one of these strange incidents that you don't know what had caused it.

I remember that we had to walk in front of the hearse from the church to the cemetery. That's what we used to do with children when they died – although she was 18 she was still considered a child. It was traumatic but, to me, in those days death was not as shocking as how it is when you are older.

For us children it was just a case that she didn't get up, so she died. The adults were confused but as children we weren't so confused about natural death but we were shocked and confused by a death that was accidental and also by the idea that you put someone in a grave and covered them with dirt. That was almost too much to bear.

Two people drowned when we were at school. It was horrendous; just shocking. Then there was the little boy who was covered in sand and another one who had a wall collapse on him and he died. They were only about seven.

One lunch time the bell rang after the lunch break and some of the boys didn't turn up and later, when some of them did arrive, they said that they were playing cricket and the ball fell into a crater and a little boy went in to get it, but there must have been some sort of landslide and he got covered in sand and died.

That was such a shock and we couldn't believe it. It stayed in the back of my head for years and years because I can bury things there and never, never go back to them. I just lock awful things away and carry on with my life.

Once, years later when my children were young, I left them with someone while I went out. When I came back, my daughter, Dian-Marie, came running up and said, "We made a swimming pool in the garden, come and see."

And when I looked they had dug a huge hole in the garden and, in a fury, I marched those children in and beat them all. The poor little things pleaded and protested, but I just whipped their behinds and didn't say a single word about why they were being punished.

I didn't explain, but what happened was that I had revisited the memory of that little boy at school who had been buried in sand all those years ago.

Of course, that was nothing to do with these children and the poor little things were completely baffled about why I was beating them. The problem was not to do with them, it was me. I was fearful about something from long ago that I had just locked away and, not knowing what else to do, I just lashed out.

Half the time when we used to beat children it was because of fear. In our heads there's a reason for chastising them but they didn't know anything about it. In a way, it's a good thing that people now have to think about the repercussions if they hit a child, although back then we thought we were acting out of love. It was a funny kind of love, in a way.

Years later, when they had grown up, I told the children what it was all about. They were confused but at least it started to make a bit of sense when I shed some light on that bizarre situation.

It had taken years for me to realise that I had been afraid something bad would have happened to them while they were digging the garden to make their 'swimming pool'.

Somewhere, in my distant memory, it had taken them a long time to get that little boy out of the hole when he was covered in sand, so he must have got stuck and suffocated. It was so horrendous.

I think I still have the sense of it in the back of my mind somewhere, and anything that triggers that memory puts me into a kind of shock: hence the over-reaction with my children and their friends that day.

That might explain why I just lock bad things away, mentally. I hate to remember awful things.

Chapter Four

Jumbies

When my mother died we moved further up to San Juan which is a few miles from Port of Spain, but to us was like the countryside.

We were now living near some old friends of my great aunt Tan-Tan, who were called Mr and Mrs Yearwood. They used to tell us all sorts of horrible stories about *Sukuya* and *Lajablesse* , which were ghosts and blood suckers.

Mr Yearwood used to warn us that cats were not the kind of animals to have as pets because they get so jealous, and, if you don't treat them right, they would creep up to you in the night and kill you.

He told us a story about how a cat climbed up on a bed where a woman was sleeping and, because she had ignored him earlier during the day, the cat stuck its tail up her nostril and she suffocated and died.

To this day I am petrified of cats because of that story. My cousins in Port of Spain knew about my fear and they threw their cat at me and it clawed me, which only compounded my phobia.

Now, if I ever go into a house and there's a cat there, nine times out of ten I can't go anywhere near it but it will come to me. When that happens, I just freeze and am rooted to the spot until it goes away or until its owner shoos it away from me.

I have friends with cats and as soon as I go to their houses they put the pet outside, otherwise I am a nervous wreck and it takes ages before I calm down.

The horror stories I had heard about cats as a child must have put that terrible fear into me. Mr Yearwood managed to convince me that, far from being harmless pets, cats were ruthless killers, and to this day I am still very frightened of them.

The old people used to do that in those days: they would tell children *jumbie* stories and frighten them. I don't know why they did that, because it was such a stupid thing to do when you think about it.

I suppose it was a way to get children to behave by scaring the life out of them and, to some extent, I suppose it worked on me because I always used to say, "I don't want to go by Mr Yearwood's because he's going to tell us all those terrible stories to frighten me."

And, yes, I would be as good as gold whenever that man's name was even mentioned.

The fear of *jumbies* was so bad that when they told those awful stories we were so disturbed and scared that we didn't even want to go from one room to the other.

And, another thing: in those days the toilets were out in the yard and in the night you would not have wanted to go to the toilet, even if you were bursting to wee-wee. You didn't want to go into the dark and risk bumping into a *jumbie*. Instead, you would use the posie – the chamber pot – underneath the bed.

I have to say that growing up was something you sort of stumbled into and so much of our childhood was fuelled by rumours, folklore, gossip, trial and error, because adults had the idea that children had no right to ask questions they considered 'impertinent' or 'precocious'.

Consequently, most of what we learned about grown up life came from whispered conversations among our peers as we huddled together to discuss things like the 'birds and bees'.

In those days, the word 'sex' was taboo and we couldn't dream of talking about things like that with grown ups.

To some extent it was even out of bounds among us children and the word was hardly ever mentioned although I started having my periods when I was about 11. Most of the girls at the school had already started, so I was quite late (I seem to be a late-comer for everything).

Why Not Me?

The day that I found out that I was having a period I was in school and I went home for lunch as usual. Afterwards, I went back to school, only to realise that my period had started. I knew I didn't hurt myself in the playground. I had a mind about what it was because the other children had talked about it, but it was not explained properly so I was a bit confused.

I simply left the school to go back home without saying anything to anybody. On the way I met one of my cousins, who asked me, "Where are you going?"

I just said, "I'm going back home, I'm going back home."

And I took off, very afraid.

She said, "But, what you going back home for?"

And I said, "Never mind, never mind, I'm just going back home."

So, I went home and Mudsy, my aunt, said to me, "What's wrong?"

And I said, "I'm bleeding."

And she just said, "All right, don't worry."

She went and got a bag with my name on it, containing sanitary diapers, and showed me what to do. Everything was well prepared in advance.

My aunt was very caring and understanding, so all the fear that I had vanished. She gave me all the information I needed but she never told me one word about sex. Never!

But the children in school did, didn't they? They told me that once you started having your period and you had sex this is going to happen and that is going to happen: "so you can't do this and you can't do that".

Yet, you know something, we never really understood about where babies came from just like how we never really understood about how Father Christmas brought Christmas presents.

The adults told you about Father Christmas and they treated sex in the same way: telling you that the stork came in the night and brought the baby. It was always in the night, never in the day, mind you, just like how Father Christmas came down the chimney in the night (although in Trinidad we didn't have chimneys).

For parents and grown-ups speaking to children about sex was unheard of, so, instead, we got our sex education from the children in the playground and it was always the same: you didn't really know the facts. It sounded rude and it sounded nasty, so we'd be saying, "*Eeeugh*, I don't want that!"

And you wouldn't want the boys to come anywhere near you because sex sounded disgusting. And when we found out what prostitutes did we would say, "How nasty, and to think they would go from one person to another!" The idea was horrible.

So, as far as sex was concerned, there was a lot to scorn and ignorance because, at one time, we even thought that if you kissed somebody you would become pregnant.

Of course, when we discovered that kissing didn't really give you babies that didn't stop us from avoiding that activity anyway because we could never be 100 percent certain. Back then, people could have told us anything and we would have believed them.

So, starting my periods was a traumatic time. Traumatic because I used to be scared of doing anything too vigorous. And, of course, I was a tomboy and prided myself on out-running, out-climbing, and out-jumping the boys, so this new rite of womanhood was cramping my style.

I became a bit subdued and feminine because they kept drilling that into me: "You're a young lady now, so behave like a young lady."

What was it they used to say? "You have to use a lot of decorum. None of that jumping and running and prancing like you used to do. You've got to be careful."

However, that didn't cut me off from playing with the boys straight away. But, when the time of the month came along, all of a sudden instead of gallivanting, I'd be keeping myself quiet over in the corner doing something else.

I was very, very skinny as a child and even when I was older I didn't have a bust. Rhona, my best friend, had an aunt who used to work in a shop called *Salvatore's* and the very first bra that I wore was from one of the mannequins in that shop because no other shop had a bra in my size. The one that Rhona brought me was a tiny, tiny bra they put on the dummy in the window display.

When I got that bra, years and years after I'd left school, I had to stuff it because I had nothing to put into it as I didn't have any breasts, just two pimples or 'heats', as my friend called them, on my chest.

In spite of that, my body never, ever bothered me. I never had a problem with being skinnier than anybody else, so it was never an issue that I happened to be thin as a rake.

I suppose I had the advantage of being able to wear some clothes that those with breasts couldn't, especially when I started out as a dancer. But, on the whole, no-one cared that I didn't have a bust, although my first choreographer used to say that I had the shape of a man: straight back and front and no hips. I was used to such comments and didn't really care.

I was never really concerned about my looks, come to think of it. Apparently people in Trinidad used to say that I was 'OK', but it has never been an issue with me. So much so that I never wore make-up, except on stage. I was not in show business because of how I looked. I have always been more interested in what I do.

I would make up my eyes because people always said, and I agreed with this, that I've got nice eyes. But I would just use petroleum jelly which I mix with an economy brand of moisturiser on my skin, and that's it.

People used to say that my grandmother was such a pretty woman but I never saw it. I suppose that was because I was just so used to seeing her. And we never had anybody in our family who loved to get up and show off. I am the most 'show off' person in my family and even I knew my limits.

As children we all did our love letters. The boy sending the letter would never say 'I am looking at you', it was always sent on behalf of somebody else and would say something like, "Thomas Moore is looking at you".

In response, the girl would say something like, "But I don't like him!" And she would make a great fuss.

Jean, was another of my best friends and she had an admirer in Arthur Goodard. When a note came telling her so Jean said, "But he's alright, you know."

I think I had a secret crush on the same boy because Arthur used to fill us up with a whole heap of stories that his uncle was Duke Ellington. And for years we really believed him.

I mean, he had a picture of the band leader at his house and he used to tell us all kinds of stories. How were we to know otherwise?

The reason we believed him was that he had an uncle called Ricky who played in the police band and he used to walk in front of the band and spin the baton and travel all over performing in various places.

What's more, when you looked at him and you looked at the picture of Duke Ellington, you could see some resemblance. So, apparently, we had this handsome guy's 'nephew' in our school and everyone fancied Arthur, especially because of his world-famous 'uncle', Duke.

And, to cap it all, Arthur lived in a family that was into show-business and artistic activities, so that made him even more appealing. But, as much as I liked Arthur and however much I day-dreamed about our future together, I knew that he and I would never kiss because I hated kissing and to this day I still don't like to kiss people. It's very strange. I never got that far with anybody until a long, long time after I had left school and was an adult.

We had boyfriends in our group but it never came to that; there was never any intimacy. We would all go out together in a group: walking and talking, but that's as far as it got.

We used to call it 'Get followed home'. All the friends would be there and they'd be giggling at the back while the girlfriend and boyfriend walked on ahead talking and feeling self-conscious.

A boy and a girl could get to snatch a little time alone when we had fairs or special occasions like that. Then, afterwards, the boy would walk the girl home and stand by the gate and talk for hours until their parent or guardian would say to her, "Don't you think it's time to come in?"

The pair would part reluctantly and spend the rest of the evening dreaming about each other.

Those were nice days, actually. Sometimes the boys from the other schools would come and hang around our school looking for girls to talk to. There was a boy called Poynts from one of the high schools. He used to come around Jean and me and try to play us off against each other. After he left we used to giggle and gossip about him: "Stupid guy, he thinks he's so nice!"

In those days we had a lot of live music everywhere, especially jazz and calypso, and we all loved to hear songs from Frank Sinatra, Ella Fitzgerald and people like that. Their songs had a lot of meaning and we would write out the words to all the popular songs in our journals.

We had a lot of choirs that we joined. The Anglican and Catholic churches always had choirs and back then the congregation didn't sing the hymns, the choirs did, but that changed later on.

There was one song that was very popular: *No-one Knows That Heavenly Dark-eyed Susan Brown*. I used to shimmy down when we sang that.

In my school days I sang but I didn't dance. I did a lot of plays and lots of singing, especially in the school choir while Myrna was in a proper choir outside of school. We sang a lot of classical songs in our choir while as friends together we would do more contemporary songs.

My family used to say that I had a voice like a silver paper over a comb, which was a compliment in those days, believe it or not. We do these back-handed compliments in Trinidad where it sounds like they're taking the mickey but they're actually complimenting you. I suppose it's a way to keep you humble. And they used to ask me to sing because my voice had a high, sweet quality to it.

We were very influenced by American style and fashion and we used to make our own clothes based on the styles we saw in shops and in magazines. We would go window shopping or we'd look in the fashion books and pick out a particular style then get someone to make the garment for us. Everybody sewed in those days, although there were proper seamstresses that you could commission.

We wore tiered or flared skirts with a crinoline underneath and tight tops. I never wore sleeveless dresses, 'armhole dresses' as we called them; I always had to have sleeves.

Straight skirts were only for adults while children wore flared skirts. Socks were for school but were never worn after school, and I never wore stockings; my legs were always bare.

I always wanted to be a teacher. From when I was a child that was all I dreamed about. I had friends who were older but I always wanted to take the little ones out and take care of them, so I suppose that's what made me interested in being a teacher.

And the children used to take to me as well, so that confirmed it. I would not have been able to be a nurse because I was very scornful and hated the idea of people being sick around me. In school we used to talk endlessly about what we wanted to do when we grew up. We were forever painting rainbows in our minds

We had a girl at school called Joan, who was a year older than us and she used to come to school wearing extremely short skirts and we didn't exactly approve of her and so we used to say she was a 'sport', which wasn't a nice word to use at that time. It was someone who was not quite a prostitute but a slut, nonetheless. I don't think she went with guys but she was a tease and used to wear tight, short clothes.

To really rub our faces in it, she was quite voluptuous and we thought she was rude because the rest of us were quite skinny and didn't have any shape to write home about. We decided that she looked a bit too "yukky for our school".

Although she was in Woodbrook, where we lived, she lived all the way down on the wrong side of the tracks, as far as we were concerned. We were very snobby. Trinidadians are, on the whole.

She wasn't our type to begin with and then she ended up dressing in a way that we didn't approve of. But she was bright and had lots of friends.

I think we might have been a bit jealous although we didn't admit it at the time. She also had a lot more freedom than we did. For example, she was out a lot later than we were allowed to be. We had to be in by six o'clock and we would hear the next day that Joan was out until eight o'clock and she was "flaunting her short clothes", and so on.

I think she achieved something and ended up quite all right in the end, although I never heard much about her once we'd left school. Secretly, some of us might have expected she would have become something scandalous or ended up in ruins but she turned out all right.

Another thing that happened in school was that the father of a boy called Chonsie got into a lot of trouble and ended up in prison. The father, an Indian, was well off and his son used to come to school wearing lots of jewellery. The father owned a nightclub where someone was killed and he ended up going to prison. This happened when Chonsie was still at school and, years later, when he tried to get into the priesthood, they wouldn't let him because of his father's past reputation.

Eventually, when the father was released he became a street preacher. They say he had found religion in jail. Some people went to see and hear him out of curiosity and others were quite cynical about whether he really had found redemption, but I believe that if someone does something wrong and they've been punished, then that's it, they've paid their dues and should have a chance to move on with their lives.

Chapter Five

War

I was just finishing my schooling when World War Two ended. My enduring memory is that my mother hadn't lived to see that war, as she herself had desired or predicted.

I sometimes think we should be careful what we wish for, because she had expressly stated that she wouldn't like to live to see another big war. Well, her wish was granted, although that left us bereft.

I suppose the most obvious effect of the war was that some of the people we knew were no longer around. Many people had enlisted and gone off to England or Canada as volunteers in the services, or had relocated elsewhere to try and improve their chances during those difficult times.

Gordon Douglas, whose sister Joyce had gone to primary school with us, was one of those people who went off to fight for the 'Motherland', as we called Great Britain. I'm not sure what he actually did for the war effort, but years later he ended up working as a cameraman for ITV, the independent television network which was a rival to the BBC.

There was a great deal of pride that we, in Trinidad, were in some way contributing to the role Britain was playing in that terrible conflict. We knew what the war was about in the sense that a lot of Americans appeared in our country and they took our best bits of land for their military bases and that sort of thing. And, of course, there were shortages: queues for provisions and rationing which we had to get used to.

People were lining up for food and all sorts of things, even coal, which was used for the coal fires. Just about everything we had previously taken for granted was in short supply, although alternative goods, some familiar and some not so well-known, would appear from Canada, Great Britain, Argentina, New Zealand, and the USA.

As far as everyday life was concerned, we weren't too badly affected. I suppose as children we weren't really aware or bothered although we did notice the queues and things. Suddenly, people had to stand in line for just about everything they wanted to buy or 'trust' on credit.

Nearly every family had their slate with the Chinese or Indian grocer and from time to time would obtain goods up to a certain point and settle the account at an agreed period. That system helped many people out of a bad patch when money was tight.

We had air raid signals and black-outs and the loud, blaring noise of the air raid warning over the tannoy would petrify young and old alike and send us flying for cover inside the nearest building. I think if we children were at our house or the house of a friend we would rush underneath a bed and lose ourselves in story-telling to take our minds off the danger outside.

But, really, during the war everything seemed to be about the Americans who were deployed to the island. Their presence amongst us made people aware that something was happening and it gave some people a better lifestyle because lots of things had to be arranged especially for the Yanks. They got the first and best of everything that was going and those locals who were close to those foreign 'guests' managed to clean up as well. On top of that, certain foods and other commodities were brought over for them by boat and, as a result, many of our people also benefited.

Suddenly we had chocolates, chewing gum, and sweets – candy – that we didn't have before in the shops, like Cadbury's chocolate, although, it wouldn't surprise me if that brand came to Trinidad from the UK *via* the USA.

The more outgoing of the women managed to get hold of stylish and colourful clothing, panty hose and fashion magazines; and the local men were more than glad to get their hands on swing records, razors, hair cream and, of course, American cigarettes and posters of movie stars.

So, in a way it was not too bad and the idea of war was not such a frightening thing for us children, probably because we didn't witness any combat. From time to time we heard our parents talking about the war but it didn't really affect our lives.

We children didn't really listen to the wireless; that was for the older people who would listen to Churchill's broadcasts and discuss those things away from our earshot. I was really glad because they would send us out to play at those times and so we were really grateful to Winston Churchill for that.

In the area where we lived there was a young offenders' institute and close by was a camp with a lot of Jewish refugees living there. We used to call it the 'containment camp' because the men there were contained and not free to come and go as they pleased. It was a bit regimental, but not like a prison camp or anything like that; more like a hostel.

A few of the residents used to come up to our house and my aunt would provide tea for them, but apart from that we didn't have any contact with those refugees. I don't think they used to work. The boys at the young offenders' place used to carry out errands for them.

Our soldiers went away and we expected them to be courageous and to come back home in one piece. And, in school, we used to make things for the War Effort Box or drop our pennies in the collection tin. While at home we were encouraged to say our nightly prayers and make mention of our brave soldiers, the war widows and orphans, and the families left behind by those fighting on the side of good against tyranny.

There was no whispering or efforts to send the children out to play when news came over the wireless that the war was over. They more or less shouted that news from the rooftops. It felt to us as exciting as the anticipation of Christmas or our birthday, although on a daily basis we didn't see any real change straight away.

The main difference after the war was that people were lifting their spirits with carnival on the streets for the first time. Rationing was coming to an end, but didn't end straight away, although after a while the Yankees went back home – thank goodness.

While they were around they were both a blessing and a curse, but I think by the end of the war most people were glad to see the back of them. Some Americans stayed on and they kept the land that they had taken over for their military bases. I think that is still a big issue of contention even today.

To children like me they were a nuisance because while they were around we were kept indoors like prisoners and could only dream of a return to our carefree days of skylarking up and down outside. Now, at last, slowly but surely, we were able to return to those days of freedom when we were no longer shut up inside fearing an air raid at any moment.

Among the few who missed those Yankees were 'the naughty people', like the prostitutes and spivs who we called 'the rats'. They were the ones who entangled themselves with the Americans, and the older generation would frown about it and mutter to each other: "Birds of a feather does flock together".

The Mighty Sparrow, the calypsonian, had a big hit record called *Jean and Dinah* which summed up that situation really humorously. It told the story of how local girls who had gravitated to the Yankees and made money from prostitution during the war were now back on the market, so to speak. The only difference was that now fellows could get them for free!

There was a place near the wharf where, just like the four-legged variety, the two-legged female 'rats' used to hang out and they would come out at night. There were loads of calypsoes about that, although Sparrow's was probably the most popular.

I also remember Lord Kitchener singing a calypso called *Mount Olga*, back then. Kitchener's proper name was Aldwyn Roberts and he was a very tall, dark, handsome man who always wore a hat and had a sort of twinkle in his eyes which made you think: don't let him see you doing anything dubious otherwise he would sing about it and everyone would know your secrets.

In those days calypsonians were accessible because they had day jobs like anybody else, so they weren't full-time singers who were really up there on a pedestal.

In Trinidad show-business was not an occupation; all performers had to have a job or a trade of some sort during the day and they would sing or play music at night or at the weekend. No-one really never made a living out of show-business back then but I think the situation is a lot different today.

The first time that we had the steel pans on the street was after the war. During October we had VJ Day (Victory in Japan) and a lot of exciting things happened. Kitchener produced a calypso about it with the lyrics: "Just try and remember, the 10th of October..."

There was also a swanky Chinese Club, *The Casual Club*, where all the upper-class Chinese and the white people went. The Maple and Malvern were the clubs where our set, the middle-class Woodbrook people, would dress up to the nines and go to party.

The lower-class people couldn't go there; that was not for them. In turn, we weren't allowed to go to the white people's clubs, although they had blacks in their clubs working as musicians and servants. Those white clubs made an exception for black celebrities or upper-class blacks who would be allowed to go to those elite venues that were designated for whites only.

Our society was very much divided along colour and class lines, and people had to know their place. The whites were looked up to, Indians and Chinese kept to themselves and were looked upon as enterprising – they were always running little businesses and handling money in one way or another, so they were respected. And virtually everyone, especially the upper class and middle-class black and brown people, looked down on the blacks who were poor.

Chapter Six

Ling

When I left school I always wanted to be a teacher and thought I would go to teacher training college straight away, but I actually went to a commercial school called Hacketts, where we learned to do typing, shorthand and book-keeping.

It was a technical college and you had to do that before you went to look for a job. Not only that, but, traditionally, when most people from Woodbrook left school they went into the civil service because that was considered the best thing to do. Or, if they had the qualifications and ability, they studied to become a doctor or lawyer.

However, even if you weren't such a high-flier, because you came from Woodbrook and were considered 'middle-class', you didn't want to 'dirty your hands' by doing trades like carpentry or plumbing, so you tried to position yourself in the civil service or in another clerical area.

I went to commercial school so I could become a typist or clerk in the civil service but, really, I had always wanted to teach. I completed my technical training but afterwards I didn't go into the civil service. Instead, I went to work as a typist with a printing company.

It was around this time that I started dancing and joined Geoffrey Holder's troupe, *The Geoffrey Holder Dance Company*, when I was 18.

Geoffrey and his brother, Boscoe, were extremely talented and were at the forefront of the arts movement in Trinidad at that time. Of course, later on they became almost legendary figures, (up to the time of Boscoe's passing), and rightly so.

What was remarkable was the way they embraced so many different aspects of the arts, from dance and drama to fine art painting and photography. I suppose the word is 'cutting edge'; they were so far ahead of their time.

Both of them had their fingers on the pulse of what was happening in the arts and they were creating new directions for local artistes, but they could also tap into what was going on abroad as well.

Like me, they were from a middle-class family with four children from Port of Spain. Boscoe, who was older, had started a dance group and, when he travelled to London, Geoffrey took over the running of the company which he was a member of as well. Between them they had so much talent that it was a seamless take over when Boscoe left to go abroad in about 1948.

When I started dancing, my grandmother was very unhappy about my decision but I was extremely stubborn and nothing would have stopped me from following my heart and doing what I enjoyed. At that time, I liked nothing more than dancing, especially because it was opening up a whole new world and connecting me with like-minded people.

Granny was very, very upset because in those days people used to say, 'No nice girls ever went on the stage'. But I wanted to go on stage even if that meant I wouldn't be considered a 'nice girl'.

As far as granny and those other older people were concerned, it was all well and good to get up on the table at home and perform as a child but another thing altogether to go on stage to do it for a living. But, if you think about it, if they hadn't allowed me to get up on the table and show off when I didn't know any better, I wouldn't have wanted to go on the stage later on, would I?

I didn't learn to dance in a conventional way. In fact, my dancing career began almost by accident. What happened was that my cousin Joyce had joined the Holder dance group and one day I was walking along the street with her and Geoffrey was in a shop and saw us.

He came out to speak to Joyce and this impressively handsome man, towering above us at 6' 6", asked me if I would come and sit for him because, as well as being a dancer and choreographer, he also used to do a lot of painting and photography.

He couldn't help but catch your eye because he was so tall and good looking, but I was quite tickled that he actually wanted me to model for him. I just took it in my stride and agreed. It was something to break up the monotony of everyday life, I suppose.

I had no idea then that something wonderful and life-changing could come out of that rather frivolous activity of just sitting and posing while you had your photograph taken.

Geoffrey used to enter and win a lot of photography competitions and he used to do everything right there in his house, which was divided into his studio and darkroom, and the living area. At that time he had a day job with the custom's service.

Anyway, Geoffrey asked if I would come and sit for him again and again, and I did. Whenever he was doing a portrait he would dress you up, put on your make-up and fix your hair. He did everything, and his mother, whom we called Mother Holder, would come and help him to transform you.

She would pluck your eyebrows, style your hair or do some of the other finishing touches. By the time they finished with you, you went from looking and feeling like the ugly duckling to feeling like you were a beautiful swan. Geoffrey was very creative and he had this amazing vision of how to transform the ordinary into a thing of wonder and beauty.

So, he took these pictures of me that first day and, as far as I was concerned, that was that, and I went back from time to time for him to do some more portraits.

One day he said to me, "Why don't you dance?"

That's how I started dancing. Interestingly, at that point he hadn't even seen me dance. I hadn't auditioned for him or anything like that. He just had an instinct, I suppose, and it turned out to be spot-on because, not only was I interested in dancing, but I was told that I was a pretty good 'shaker'.

Some time after that, a photograph that he took of me was published in a magazine and won a competition in Venezuela.

I was very vain in those days so I felt good about being the centre of attention, and it gave me more ammunition to show off with.

Not too long after I joined Geoffery's troupe we were taken to Puerto Rico for a festival and that was fabulous. We used to perform all over Trinidad but going abroad was just so exciting. Travel really does broaden the mind and going abroad as a performer really boosted my confidence and made the group of us feel special, as though we were cultural ambassadors or something exceptional like that. We were representing our country, after all.

We met so many different young people who, like us, were starting out in their careers and with the war behind us it felt as though we were entering a whole new era where the world belonged to the young, the daring, the cultured and the beautiful.

The majority of the artistic people in dance were gay at that time but we had more women in the troupes because the men were scared to join for fear of being labelled 'queer'.

Back in the old days, homosexuality was considered a bit of a scornful thing and people kept away from those who were openly gay. As far as society was concerned, homosexuality was taboo so a lot of gay people hid their sexuality, although some were quite flamboyant and you knew about it or guessed but you didn't dare say anything. Some, the minority, were open about it although a lot of gay men also had wives and lived a double life.

It was thought that it was only 'queers' that danced – they used to call gay men 'queers' back then.

Some people thought nothing of saying things like, "What are you doing in a dance group, are you queer or something?"

That's what they used to ask the young men who danced with us. But, of course, women used to get away with becoming dancers because dancing was considered feminine and a man dancing was therefore seen as effeminate.

Very seldom did you find lesbian women in troupes but you did find gay men and even up to now parents are nervous of sending their boys to do ballet because of the fear of them being labelled as gay, as though it's not possible to be graceful and artistic without being gay.

We were mainly doing folk dancing and traditional local dances mixed in with modern dance, which was very new and creative.

Nothing like that had been done before and, in fact, some of the old folk dances were more or less dying out so by reviving them with a new, modern twist we were breathing life in our traditional forms.

We wore lots of flouncy, beautiful costumes with big circular skirts for many of our performances. Sometimes, our heads were tied in that old-fashioned style the way women used to dress in the olden days, and the male dancers were often topless and dressed in simple pants looking like feckless country boys.

I became famous for doing a dance called the *Shango*, which Geoffrey choreographed especially for me. I became known as *The Shango Dancer* for doing that wild, frenetic folk dance, which became a popular fixture in our repertoire.

Geoffrey called me 'Ling', from the word lingé, because I was tall and very, very skinny: all arms and legs. I was like a twig and up into my twenties had the body of a school girl.

I only had two or three years dancing with Geoffrey before he left to go to the United States, then we had a woman choreographer called Marie Jean François.

She was born in Trinidad and went away to America where she trained under Katherine Dunham. Later, she decided to form a troupe back home in Trinidad, which is why she returned.

Marie Jean was a very tall, leggy and attractive woman with freckles and she wore a lot of jewellery, so these things were always jangling as she moved. She was very flamboyant, really theatrical and over the top.

Her second-in-command was a woman called Cecile Ford, one of our leading artistes in Trinidad, a very bright woman and a beautiful singer. She eventually went to Germany as a singer and did very well, I believe.

I danced with Madame Marie for a while and went with the troupe to Curacao, Martinique, Venezuela and Barbados and before she went abroad again. After that, my dancing was put on hold for a while before I travelled to England in the mid-50s, but I'll come to that.

As I said, my training was not conventional. It was never a question of going to a dancing school to learn to dance. With both Geoffrey and Marie we learned as we danced, so our training was on the hoof (so to speak) and integrated into the performances.

Geoffrey did everything himself but Madame Marie had an assistant, and with both companies we did shows all over Trinidad. The dance groups were mixed and there were about 30 of us, including the musicians. Being on the road made us a close unit and in time we were so close that we were like a family.

People would envy us for being in those groups, especially when they were stuck at home doing an ordinary job or working in a trade that neither allowed them to see the world nor receive the applause of appreciative crowds.

My grandmother was never among those appreciative crowds, however. She never came to see me perform and remained upset and disappointed that I had stubbornly stuck to my guns in choosing a career as a dancer – although in some ways the career seemed to have chosen me since I didn't plan it.

The chance to dance came my way, I took it and the rest is history. Anyway, although she was displeased, my grandmother didn't forbid me from doing it.

If she had prevented me and really put her foot down then I probably would have stopped, I don't know, but since she didn't insist, I carried on. In hindsight, that was probably the best decision I have ever made.

Chapter Seven

Carnival and Pan Power

Music and dancing have always been a part of me. I grew up with those elements all my life and because I was born on a carnival Sunday, that more or less confirmed my love of both.

The history of the carnival was very interesting. The slaves had a festival called Camboulé which dated back to slavery when they used to cut the cane and after that they were given a rest day when they would get drunk and carry on with their festivities.

The French aristocrats had a lot of masked balls back then. When the slaves became free what they did was to have their carnival around Easter time where they would dress up and parade and mimic the slave owners and aristocrats. There was a lot of debauchery, but on the Ash Wednesday the people went to church and confessed their sins.

After Palm Sunday everyone would go to church and get palm branches at the service, carry those back to the church and they would burn those to ashes. On Ash Wednesday the priest would use the ashes to mark the sign of the cross on their foreheads.

Although carnival was, and is, such a big event in Trinidad, up to today it is not a public holiday, it's a 'privilege day', which means time off is granted rather than being compulsory.

Children would go to school when carnival was going on, but most times we would get a half day off. At first children didn't play mas but some children did put on disguises and then later on more children would get involved.

At first the bands weren't on the road, they were on trucks and they used to have characters like devils and 'jab-jabs', which were like demons with orks, and burrokeets, - little donkeys.

Nowadays, they have an archive exhibition where they show you the old-time masks and how things used to be in the old days going back to when the festival first began.

Back then, a lot of our parents didn't play mas, either. For example, my grandmother would never even go to town on a carnival day. She was very adamant that she didn't approve of the bacchanal and she used to stay home.

I think the proud, old people frowned on it and thought it was lewd behaviour. We children thought it was wonderful and couldn't wait for carnival to come around.

We wouldn't be able to sleep the night before a carnival. We had something called J'ouvert, which means 'opening the day', and people would come out in costume disguises on that first day of the festivities.

We called it a 'disguise dance'. I would go into town with my aunt and the others and it was very exciting: lots of colour, crowds, spectacle, noise and wonderful food.

We used to have Discovery Day – celebrating the day Columbus 'discovered' Trinidad, where the police bands and the other classical brass bands would come out and have a parade.

And we had Empire Day and the schools got a tin of chocolate with a picture of the king on it and some other little treats. We would march up to the savannah and listen to the Governor General making a speech about our place in the Commonwealth of Nations. We felt very proud.

The Red Cross was always present at things like that just in case there were any small accidents or incidents brought on by high spirits or whatever.

I was introduced to Lord Kitchener one year. I went to the calypso tent and saw him there, although, being middle-class and from the more upmarket part of Woodbrook, we weren't allowed to socialise with people like that. They didn't come from Behind the Bridge, which was the poor, shanty town area where the so-called lower-class people lived, but they didn't come from the elite, either.

In any case they could have been living among us but it still wouldn't make any difference because they were not in our class so they would have come under the same heading as the steel bands.

Those were the people who were expected to associate with 'the rats' and, funnily enough, the white people would have gone to the calypso tents and made friends with the calypsonians but we wouldn't. The whites were more open but some of our set were stuck up and thought themselves better than some other people.

Now, the calypso tent – we called it a tent but it wasn't really a tent – it was an event held in a cinema, especially the Empire Cinema, or another location like that. Nowadays, they actually have tents – a hall specially shaped like a tent, but it's really a building that has been decorated and is open 24-7 that they adapt and use for calypso performances and other entertainment.

The calypsoes were always there – even before I was born but many people make the mistake of linking the emergence of the steel bands with the calypsoes. No, the bands came along afterwards but the calypsoes were always there. They started in slavery days when the people wanted to communicate with one another but were forbidden by the slave masters because of the restrictions and repressions, so they would sing and pass on messages that way.

The slave masters must have thought they were just singing happy songs, but in fact they were plotting and scheming and sending codes to one another.

As time went on, they started making calypsoes on different themes. Then they had something called picong, which comes from the Spanish or the French and means 'teasing'. That's when they make up a song about you for a joke, and you retaliated and so it goes on.

They used to have tents where people just did this picong thing. We always say that the Jamaicans can't take picong; they're too sensitive and take the jokes personally and get too bad-tempered and upset, but we Trinis just take it as a joke and we could sit down all night not singing but talking and 'pulling each other's legs'. They still have that but they don't call it picong any more, they call it Extempo now.

Calypso started out of that, and it's not something new and they always did calypsoes about things that were happening in the society. It was like singing the news. It was never about make believe; it was always real and it remains that way. So, public figures and celebrities who are conceited and stuck-up can find themselves pulled down to earth when they get sent up in a calypso. It can be very degrading.

I always say that I go to Trinidad and visit the calypso tents because I would always get to find out what was happening in the country. I don't have to read the newspapers to find out what is going on, and because Trinidadians make a joke of everything. They never take things seriously, so that was always a good way to ease the tension. That's what calypsoes used to be about and it's still that way: calypsoes are social commentary.

The Mighty Sparrow (Slinger Fransico) made quite an impression from his first calypso when he was known as Little Sparrow in the early 1950s. Then, as Mighty Sparrow, he won the Road March and Calypso Monarch crown with *Jean and Dinah*, and the rest is history.

Calypso was the sort of art form that would unite everybody and the steel bands used to promote the same kind of vibe. But our set wouldn't dare fraternise with calypsonians otherwise it would have been frowned upon.

Our associates would have said, "What is she doing talking to a steel band man or calpsonian?"

It was totally taboo, except for the steel band in Woodbrook because those guys used to go to school with us. We used to talk to them (eventually), that much was permitted because they were from among us, but the town boys used to come up to fight them.

There were big band wars going on and lots of developments as the bands became more and more popular and more competitive as the craze grew. It took off even to the point that Ellie Mannet, who used to beat the first pan with the Invaders Steel Band, actually used to read music and he was one of the first trained musicians to play in a steel band. I think he used to tune the pans for his own band, the Oval Boys, in our part of Woodbrook.

The bands all had big pan yards to practice in. In those days, it was about two houses that would join up and allow practice and performances to go on in the yards, but now it's more open and they have a little shop where they sell curios, refreshments and other little bits and pieces.

This music and culture is so much part of me, because I grew up with it more or less from day one. My family on both sides were immersed in music, although that was more classical forms, and some of us played instruments (one of my uncle played the sax and piano, another played the trumpet, and a nephew played the violin). And we were always singing, so, a love of music was always there. Adopting a love of the pan music was just a natural thing for us.

Who would have thought that music could be transformed into another sphere that no-one knew anything about? Who would have imagined that something called 'Pan' that had never existed before would emerge and make such a big impression? That sort of innovation created great excitement, and it started in Trinidad. Who knew that we could do that?

We knew we could play music and perform on instruments like the trumpet, saxophone, piano, drums and so on, but to develop another instrument – the steel pan – to add to that was just wonderful.

All of a sudden, there was a pan to go with the collection of other musical instruments. Isn't it amazing that something dirty and discarded like an oil drum could be cleaned up and re-designed into a musical instrument that is now played in steel orchestras throughout the world?

At first, the elite used to look down on the people who played the pan, but they never really looked down on the pan itself, you know; they enjoyed the music.

When I first came up to the UK it was around February or March when carnival is held in Trinidad. I missed it so much that I remember saying to Trevor, "Gosh, I can hear the steel pan beating in my head".

The Trinidad carnival was calling me from across the miles.That was the first carnival that I had missed and it happened around the same time as I emigrated. But it was as though I could sense the vibrations; that connection was still with me because long after the steel bands have gone you can still 'hear' that music in your head: you feel it deep inside your soul.

I play mas every year when I go back to Trinidad but I would never play in a music band; I always play in a steel band. The rhythm is a different sort of rhythm and I can feel that rhythm in my body. The music band doesn't give me that same sort of feeling.

When I was about 14 years-old they had a dance called the 'jerk waist' (*'juck waist'*), which was quite suggestive. My girlfriend Jean Furlong had a brother who used to run out of school as soon as class was finished to go to the steel band yard to play the pan. He must have been only about 12 or 13 but he used to learn all the different dances, including the 'jerk waist', and come to show Jean and me how to do them.

If my grandmother knew I was doing those dances, especially the 'jerk waist', she would have had a fit! It's a dance where your waist goes from side to side in rhythm with the music. I suppose it looked very sexual and that's probably why the old people objected to those dances.

I did the dance one night a few years ago and I was there with the dancer Greta Mendez, and she was there whining up on the dance floor and carrying on, so I got up and started doing the 'jerk waist' and she cried out, "Oh, gosh, Corinne Skinner, you know how long I haven't seen that dance?"

So, all that time ago Jean's brother used to teach us the moves and Jean and I would be winding down and carrying on bad while the others looked at us and were green with envy because we knew the latest moves.

Interestingly, the same thing that I'm complaining about now with the young people of today grinding down and doing all sorts of sensuous dancing is the same thing I was doing when I was a girl, only not so blatantly. At least I'd like to think so, but one difference – we never dared do our whining down in public, only for fun amongst ourselves.

We became very interested in the steel bands when they first started, although we weren't allowed to be involved because that was considered to be a social thing for people who came from Behind the Bridge, which was considered a place of low-class culture.

At first, we used to snub the Oval Boys, our local Woodbrook band as well because there were about two or three members who came from Behind the Bridge in that band, although the rest were considered 'decent' Woodbrook boys. But, over time, we dropped our reservations and started to speak to them and became very supportive and saw them as 'our band'.

To start with, the steel bands were very basic. Back in those days, they made music out of two pieces of bamboo – what we called 'bamboo-tamboo'. But then they started to improve and we became very proud of those people who could take up an old dustbin and make music out of it.

The people in Trinidad are very artistic and we are proud of people who are creative, whatever the art form. As long as they can make something good, we can appreciate what they are trying to achieve.

So, although playing the pan was what the poorer class would have done, the very elite person would have seen the potential and would appreciate that there was something good to come out of that culture: from 'bamboo-tamboo' to the crude (excuse the pun) drum pans, and from that to steel bands and orchestras. You could see the progression.

Anyway, although to begin with we may have scorned the people who were doing it, we would have appreciated what they were doing. And you could see that it was because of the lack of resources that they were so creative. That's when you could see what the peasants could do.

Those people mainly stayed home; they were not doing anything else like going out to work, so they amused themselves and were very creative and artistic, and what they produced was a stroke of genius.

They invented the steel band and that's greatest musical invention of the twentieth century, in my opinion. As you know, those pans can play anything and everything. The only sad thing about that is that we didn't get it patented and a lot of people have been complaining about that because pan is all over the world and all sorts of people are making the claim that they invented pan. That is an insult to our heritage.

It's like our calypsoes that they took to America and made famous, although they had other people singing them. They had hit songs like *Rum and Coca Cola* and they claimed that calypso music originated in America when it didn't.

Harry Belafonte did some Kitchener calyposoes and did quite well. Harry was just in the right place at the right time and he was very handsome and very good, I must say, but he's not a calyposian. People like Sparrow and Shadow are real calypsonians.

In Trinidad, St Clair, north-west of Port of Spain, was where all the white people lived. Woodbrook was the place where the middle-class people came from, and Behind the Bridge was really the place for working-class and lower-class people.

I was from Woodbrook and we were kept away from people who lived Behind the Bridge. They were considered uncouth and everyone looked down on them. They were rough, nasty, low types and we used to use the term 'Rab' to describe them. In hindsight, it was a nasty, condescending way of describing fellow human beings and we had no right to be so offensive.

People from Behind the Bridge were considered to be from the 'wrong side of the tracks' and we wouldn't mix with them. But that led to a rather strange thing as far as our school was concerned because a lot of the children who were top in our classes were from Behind the Bridge.

They were extremely bright kids and we also had a headmaster called Mr Grandison and he taught in a school that was Behind the Bridge. He was like a tyrant and all those boys who came out of his class went to the top schools and colleges – he ruled them with a rod of iron and brought out the brilliance in them.

Circumstances had located them Behind the Bridge, but people from there weren't all dunces any more than our set were all top-flight scholars. There were also many businessmen who had shops and enterprises Behind the Bridge. The father of one of my good friends owned about three shops there. In those days, 70 percent of the shops were Chinese or Indian.

We had a lot of bright kids from that part of the town and when Trinidad became independent Eric Williams, the Prime Minister, made sure that those people weren't forgotten like before and some of them were involved in his cabinet. They were just as important as anyone else it's just that they were living on the wrong side of the street, as far as we were concerned, although I'm sure some of them were better off than some of us.

We knew quite a few guys who married girls from that area and their families were very disappointed with it but there was nothing they could do. No guy or girl would be cut off by their family, but the relatives would show their displeasure. They would make the person concerned feel uncomfortable, and that was a form of rejection, really.

I knew a lot of people who, even today, will not say that they had come from Behind the Bridge, whereas some others are proud of the fact.

It is a caste and class thing and, for some, the taboo is still there up to today. Although, if we are thinking clearly about it we would see, like Martin Luther King said, that people should be judged on the basis of their character and not according to colour, caste, what they do or don't do for a living, or where they live.

Chapter Eight

Is this Love?

Although I was doing a great deal of dancing and travelling abroad to perform, I still had to be working in a 'proper job' as a clerical assistant at a printing company.

There's no need to ask what I enjoyed doing more out of the two, but that's just how it was. Dancing may have been my passion but it didn't give me a livelihood, so I had to have a day job which brought money into the house.

It was around this time that I started to get quite serious with a guy called Clifford. He and I had started going around together from the time I was at Modern Secondary and he used to go to St Mary's, one of the local colleges.

We were very friendly with his family and one of his sisters, Eileen, was in the same class as me and was a good friend. At that point we had moved from Port of Spain to Barataria. The American military had an air base at Wallafield and closed down the young offenders' institute and Papa Carr, my uncle, who was the chief officer there, retired and bought a place in Barataria, so we went to live there.

Clifford lived in the next block from our house and we became friends. Sometimes we would travel to school together on the train. As we became more intimate he started to become possessive and decided that he wanted me to stop dancing.

Now, I can become very obstinate if people try to make me do what I don't want to do. Clifford was worse than my grandmother and he kept on about it until, finally, I relented and stopped dancing. I think he was very pleased with himself. I was now the perfect, controllable girlfriend so he felt in charge, I suppose.

However, one day Geoffrey Holder came to me and said, "Ling, I've got the best dance for you – the best dance ever!"

And he started showing me all the steps and he was very excited and then, remembering that I was under Clifford's embargo, he said, "You don't have to come to rehearsals; I'll come up here and show you how to do the dance."

So that's what we did and I was enjoying this but Clifford didn't know about it. The next thing you know my picture was in the papers, splashed over the evening news saying that I was going to perform a special dance that Geoffrey had devised for me.

Clifford turned up clutching the newspaper in a fuming temper and asked me, "What's this about you doing a dance? We agreed that you weren't going to do that any more."

I told him, "You agreed, I didn't agree."

He tried to talk me out of it but I refused to change my mind. I did my dance, which was a storming success. I really threw myself into the role; flailing my body and shaking like I was possessed. The dance was a sort of reference to the Shango religion which some people in Trinidad belonged to, like the Shango Baptists, which has a strong African influence.

I loved doing the dance and really enjoyed the reaction and thunderous applause after I finished on stage, out of breath but exhilarated.

After that reaction, there was no turning back. It was from all that that I went to Puerto Rico with the troupe to perform in a cultural festival.

Clifford was just about a year older than me and his sister Eileen and I were very close. I was moving with him but I don't think I was in love with him, even though he was in love with me.

A long time ago that I discovered that I don't think I ever loved anybody. I don't think I did for the simple reason that I can do without anybody. I will do what I want to do and I have been pressing within myself to find out about this word 'love', and I've concluded that I don't understand the meaning of that word, just like I don't understand the word 'depression'.

I don't understand the word in the sense that – and I don't think I'm a cold person – it takes me a long time to get attached to anybody, number one, and when I get attached to them it doesn't take me that long to get detached.

And I don't go to bed thinking, "Oh, he's gone or she's gone or it's gone." I don't get attached to anything; absolutely anything. So I'm coming to the conclusion that I don't think I've ever loved anybody in that deeply committed and co-dependent sense of the term and I don't get emotional about a lot of things.

I have been trying to analyse myself recently and I think it all stems from my upbringing. With no mother and no father around (he was living in America), just a grandmother and various aunts, I think I learned to become emotionally detached and self-contained. That's probably why I am the way I am in that regard.

Things upset me but don't unsettle or destabilise me; things are of the moment and as soon as the moment's gone, I'm on to something else. I don't allow things to stay there and fester, I just let it go. It's not just me; none of my family that I know of are in that situation where they get emotional and worked up about things.

I have had just two boyfriends in my entire life, one of whom I married, whereas a friend of mine changes her boyfriend practically every other week and she's the one who gets jealous about this and worked up about that. But none of us in our family behave like that.

Anyway, I kept on dancing and Clifford kept on quarreling. Eileen, his sister, my best friend, had left around that time to go to England, so it was a bit traumatic for me. As friends we were always together and I missed her terribly.

She was a sprinter and had gone to England to represent Trinidad in the Empire Games, before they were called the Commonwealth Games. She was extremely good, one of the two best athletes in the country and she was expected to return home with a gold medal.

Before she left she gave me a warning, "don't you dare leave my brother, you know, because I will get vex with you!"

I didn't leave him. In fact, I got pregnant, although I didn't know that I was pregnant for a long time. I was still dancing and funnily enough I wasn't big, my bump didn't really show until way up when it was almost time to deliver.

I hardly had any stomach showing (I've probably got more stomach now than throughout the whole of my pregnancy). And because I didn't have any bottom or bust either, no-one, except close family members, had a clue that I was expecting a baby.

I gave up work when I was six months' pregnant. My aunt had this thing about me stopping sooner but my head wasn't really together so I kept going until stopping seemed the right thing to do.

One moment I was happy and the next I thought this is going to cramp my style but then the rest of the family were so nice and supportive that it was really good and I looked forward to being a mother. Clifford was excited and he wanted to get married but I didn't want to.

Our daughter, Dian-Marie, was born at eight months. It was coming up to Christmas and the Friday night before they used to have Christmas shopping night, so the shops stayed open up until about ten o'clock rather than shutting at four in the afternoon.

That evening the others went shopping but I stayed at home. I was spending time at my aunt's in Picton Street and I was sitting in a rocking chair and a cat came into the room and sat down about four feet from me. It just sat there staring at me.

As I said, I am petrified of cats and didn't dare move or rock the chair; I just froze. The cat's eyes would change colour as it blinked: one minute it was green, then it was grey, then it was blue and I was rooted to the spot while this creature sat there tormenting me with its multi-coloured eye show.

Can you imagine? The cat ain't moving and I ain't moving! And we sat there for what must have been hours. The first person that came in the door broke the stand-off and the cat scampered and I went hysterical. They could not calm me down; I just went mad and that forced me into an early labour. Dian-Marie was born at four o'clock the following morning.

In fact, two things had shocked me and induced an early labour: on the weekend before the incident with the cat we'd had a huge earthquake that and it broke the steeple at the Anglican church not far from us.

In my curiosity, I had run outside when the earth had started to shake and the woman next door had bellowed at me, "Get back inside, and don't stand up out here!"

The radio had gone off and when it did come back on they said that the earthquake was so much on the Richter scale, and it was the biggest in Trinidad's history. The following weekend they were expecting some more tremors. So the effect of that had startled me and, on top of that, being 'tortured' by that cat must have forced me into labour.

That night, before I actually went into labour, I kept going to the toilet and my aunt said, "Why are you going to the toilet so often?" and I told her I felt as though I was pushing and couldn't stop. Straight away she realised that my contractions had started. I had been booked into a clinic but because the baby was coming early they had to knock on a midwife's door a little way from our house and she came and did the delivery right there.

Dian-Marie was a little thing, weighing just four pounds. And her eyes were a lovely amber colour and I always used to tell her that she had cat's eyes.

She got those eyes, not from the cat that had petrified me the night before she was born, but from her father who is very fair-complexioned and from my own father, who has got the same light coloured eyes. When she was small her eyes were a different colour but they changed as she grew older.

I used to get up early and take her for walks around the savannah and one morning two women passed us and one peered in the pram and remarked, "You see that chile? It's a white man's chile. She must have got it from one of them white men in St Clair."

It felt good to be a mother and they used to tell me that I was showing off, but I was ready to dance as soon as they were ready for me. Clifford was proud of his baby and was always there but I didn't want to be close to him. I think I resented him in a way because I thought he was trying to bully me.

Anyone who tries that with me won't be around for long because I'm not used to being bullied. I'm used to having my own way; I can't handle that kind of controlling attitude. He wanted us to be a family, and I think he became frustrated because I didn't want to marry him.

He got married to a woman with a young child soon after Dian-Marie was born. I wasn't jealous. I just thought, "If you're going to behave like that then better you go."

I sometimes think that nobody has controlled me or impressed me emotionally enough to make me lose control of who I am or what I want to do. I let them think they're in control but they're not. I know my mind and no-one controls me.

I didn't get any grief about being unmarried and pregnant, and I could walk the street until Dian-Marie was born without any difficulty or anguish, so that was a consolation. In those days it was taboo to have a child out of wedlock, especially if you were supposed to be middle-class.

Quite a few people my age had babies by this time. Even some of our dancers had children before me, but that wasn't the point because that wasn't what my family had expected and so, in a way, that was a disappointment to them.

Close friends used to make up songs and make fun of me: "How is Genafique today?" But they were OK, it was just one of those things, I suppose.

I christened the baby when she was a month-old because she was so tiny and my family thought it was best to christen her because she might not live. Not that she was sickly or anything but she was so, so small. I don't think I'm exaggerating if I say she was about 12 inches long and weighed about four pounds.

The clothes I put on her when she was born were too big so I had to put my doll's clothes on her, which were the only garments that could fit her properly.

I had chosen people to be her godparents and then we had the christening which Clifford came to and he was so desperate to be mentioned on the christening certificate that he pleaded to be her godfather.

Eventually, I agreed and he became her godfather. I did not put his name down as the father. In those days they didn't put the father's name on the birth certificate they just put the mother's name, so, as Dian-Marie Skinner, she had my maiden name.

When Clifford came to the christening you could see that he was still anxious for us to get back together. I mean, he really did want us to be married and be a family and his attempt to be cited as a godfather was his attempt to be part of the child's life. He probably thought I would shut him out altogether otherwise.

Anyway, by that time I was getting ready to leave Trinidad. I left when Dian-Marie was six months old. It was quite an eventful time, really, because Clifford's father died before he got married and before I left the country.

Eileen, his sister, encouraged me to go to England. She was the one who first put the idea in my head and she's the one who received me when I arrived in England, she and Trevor Carter, who had emigrated in 1954, a year before I arrived there.

I had stopped working before the baby was born in any case and there was no money coming in as before. That was one thing, but in my head I knew I didn't want to go back to that job, although I was thinking about what else I might do because, of course, I had a baby to provide for.

In those days your family would keep you if you weren't working but I knew that couldn't last so something had to happen.

I got a lot of encouragement to go to England and, although my father was living in the United States, he was very supportive. He was hoping I would change my mind about going to the UK and go to America instead.

He had offered so many times before but for some reason I never wanted to go to the United States and kept declining his invitations. America was much closer and a lot of my friends and former school mates had gone there but in my long-term memory my mother died just before my ninth birthday and my father had gone there about two years before on a boat. When he came back, they had incarcerated him on the boat and he wasn't allowed to leave until they had sorted out his papers.

We had gone down to the wharf and seen him but he couldn't get off, and we couldn't get on to talk to him, but when they sorted it all out he went back to sea but in my head somewhere my mother had said she was never going to go to America, so I was never going to go to America, either.

When my father sent the first invitation, I didn't accept, and when the second one came I did the same thing. I knew I wasn't going there and so it was easy enough to make up my mind to go to England. In my head I had a good opportunity to start afresh and put the many problems I was facing behind me.

Leaving Trinidad was Plan B as opposed to Plan A, which was simply to stay home and try and get a job and balance that out with a lot of difficulty and embarrassment in trying to raise a baby as a single mother.

So, Plan B, to go to England, was the best solution, I thought. It was going to be really a new life for me. I had Eileen and Trevor waiting, so I wasn't going to be making a leap in the dark all on my own. I had a comfort zone to go to. I had in mind that I wanted to escape; to turn the page and start over in a new place.

When I left home I said I was going to start a new life and train to be a teacher. It was even in the newspapers in Trinidad that "Corinne Skinner is leaving for England where she's going to study teaching".

As usual there was no privacy. I planned to stay abroad for three years and go back home with a professional qualification so I could go into teaching and have some good prospects ahead of me when I returned home. So I thought.

At that point, Trevor Carter and I were still only friends, platonic friends, and our families were quite close. We called his aunt 'Auntie Gwennie' and she had gone to school with my Aunt Mudsy, so it's always been a family thing.

And when I came to England, I bought up things for him from his mother. We were a very close community at home and that's how we remained.

Yet, somehow, Trevor loved to tell people that he had sent for me and paid my fare to England. He'd say "I gave Corinne fifteen shillings to pay her passage."

That was his joke but in fact it was my father who paid my fare. What Trevor did do, along with Eileen, Clifford's sister, was to encourage me to make that journey.

At that time Trevor had said, "Bring Dian-Marie", but Eileen had said, "No, leave her."

And it was she that I listened to. It was traumatic not just leaving my baby behind, but leaving Trinidad, my family, friends and all I had ever known, but in my true fashion I kept all my emotions bottled up inside and did what I had to do.

I set off for England, and pastures new.

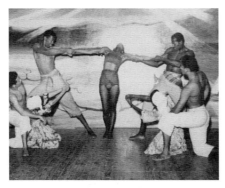

Dance diva: Corinne – 'Ling' (centre), with members of the *Geoffrey Holder Dance Company* in Trinidad. Pictured are Geoffrey (back, left), 'Popo', 'Pints', 'Popsy', 'Scogie' and Julia.
Photo: ©Geoffrey Holder

(Left) Corinne in costume with the *Geoffrey Holder Dance Company* at the start of her career as a performer.
Photo: ©Geoffrey Holder

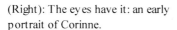

(Right): The eyes have it: an early portrait of Corinne.
Photo: ©Corinne Skinner Carter / Black Stock

(Top and Left): Corinne in a couple of her early dance roles: from the film *Cleopatra* and from the TV production *Arabian Nights* (left).
Photo: ©Corinne Skinner Carter / Black Stock

(Right): Thinking ahead: portrait of Corinne in costume for another dance role as she ponders a change of career.
Photo: ©Corinne Skinner Carter / Black Stock

(Top): Corinne, playing a
nurse, with actor Bernard
Youens as 'Stan Ogden',
in *Coronation Street.*
Photo: ©Granada.
(Above): with Norman
Beaton in *Empire Road.*
Photo: ©BBC.
(Left): In the play, *Alas,
Poor Fred* by James
Saunders.
Photo: ©Paul Armstrong.

(Top): Corinne with Peggy Phango, in a scene from *Fishing*, by Paulette Randall. Photo: ©Alex von Koett Litz
(Left): Corinne in character for another acting role, having put her dancing days firmly behind her.
(Below): Corinne at a Carnival meeting with husband Trevor Carter.
Photo: ©Errol Hill

Chapter Nine

Going to England

I spent two weeks at sea on a French boat, the *SS Columbie*, one of two boats that used to come to Trinidad. The other was the *SS Antilles*, so when one was coming one way the other was going the other way.

All the staff spoke French and we travelled around the West Indies picking up people from various places: Guyana, Grenada, and Barbados.

The food on board wasn't so nice: it was plain, whereas we were accustomed to highly-seasoned food. I mean, that type of food might be suitable to my palate now that I'm a lot older, but not back then when I thought, "My gosh, is this what we have to eat?", and I would head for the bread and butter because I just couldn't eat the meal. If only I had travelled with some hot pepper sauce everything might have been alright because that would make even the most plain dish palatable.

They served the same dry red wine with every meal and we used to put sugar in our wine to sweeten it so we could drink it, as it was too sour otherwise. In Trinidad everything we had was either very sweet or very salty. The sweet things abounded and we had condensed milk which ended up in the tea along with spoonfuls of sugar.

On the boat we had concerts and different forms of entertainment, so it wasn't too tedious. We stopped off at Barbados, where we got off and did some sightseeing and shopping and didn't stop again until we reached Spain, where we disembarked just long enough to do a little more shopping and sightseeing around the bay.

I was already a shopaholic then – and I did a bit of shopping and bought a lovely doll for Dian-Marie, which I was going to send for her.

I missed her terribly but kept telling myself that I was making the journey so that I could make a better life for her in the long run. Soon, we would be reconciled and not too long when she was no longer a little girl but soon, very soon, I told myself.

I had travelled abroad before with people I knew but this time the journey was full of complete strangers. We were all in the same boat, so to speak, because all of us were embarking on a journey of discovery and none of us knew first-hand what England would be like and what the future held for us there.

We were in sort of dormitories. There were four bunks in every room and we had to make friends, which was easy for me because I used to talk a lot. There was fun to be had with the other passengers, and making friends was a wonderful distraction to take my mind off the worries I was leaving behind and the fears you might have had about where you were going.

Our routine was to get up in the morning, dress for breakfast and then walk around the ship, play board or card games in the recreation room and go to the pool. We'd work up an appetite and then go for lunch, and in the evening we dressed for dinner. The idea of it was quite luxurious because we felt like tourists, even though we were not on a first-class ocean liner or anything as grand as that. There were some occasions when we would be invited to the captain's table, so that felt a bit special.

Once we arrived, from Plymouth we took the boat train and I remember the journey as we travelled through the open countryside to Paddington in London. We passed these fields covered in a mass of beautiful flowers, as far as the eye could see. They were daffodils: fields and fields of them, and it was extraordinary.

I'd never seen anything like it, and it lifted the spirits to see such a display of nature in full bloom. It was the first week in July 1955, the middle of summer, and although it was bright, the weather to me was still quite cold. It was perhaps very mild, warm or even hot by British standards.

I was wearing a lovely cotton suit that had been made for me and, although it looked lovely and was elegant, it was just a little too thin for the climate, especially because I wasn't used to such low temperatures.

Thankfully, the people who met me, Eileen and Trevor, had the good sense to bring a coat for me and I was very grateful because that was the first time that I was really feeling the cold. You can just imagine that coming from the constant, burning heat of Trinidad to this cool climate was a culture shock.

The sea of beautiful flowers in the fields had been the first thing that had grabbed my attention and the other feature that formed my first impression was the sight of white porters at the station when the train arrived at Paddington in London. I had never seen anything like it: white men carrying people's bags and baggage! And one of them even offered to carry mine! I never, ever expected to see such a spectacle.

Where I came from white people never did such menial work; they were always waited on by dark-skinned people and we had no idea that they could be capable of such demeaning roles. And, of course, we thought that such jobs were demeaning but we assumed it was all right for black people to do such chores. You're so stupid at that age, you didn't think. Of course the porters were white, who else would it be and why wouldn't they be doing the menial jobs in their country?

London was big, gloomy, busy, dirty, grey and a lot less glamorous and exciting than I had imagined it could ever be. I don't know what I had expected, really.

We used to hear about this big Great Britain and the monarchy, Parliament and the seat of the British Empire, so we had high expectations and grand, fanciful ideas about what this Motherland was all about. I think I expected it to be rich-looking, posh, and exclusive.

It wasn't until after arriving here that every single illusion was shattered and the cold, hard reality became clear. This may have been the land of opportunity but it was no paradise.

As I said, when I came up I bought a parcel for Trevor Carter and also one for Boscoe Holder, which their families had sent for them. In those days of course you didn't open parcels that people gave you; you just brought it up just as you'd received it, whereas nowadays you have to open them to check what you're carrying, for security reasons.

They had a meal prepared for me and made me welcome and then they took me to 35 Christchurch Hill in Hampstead, near the Heath, to meet my English landlady. She was one of Trevor's communist friends who owned the house and they had arranged for me to rent a room from her. It was the first time that I felt lonely and on my own wondering, "What am I doing here?"

That was the time when homesickness started to rear its head. There was a kitchen on the top floor which I would share with another tenant, and we shared a bathroom. Well, I wouldn't sit in the bath, I used a pail which I would fill up with water and then I used a cup to gather up the water to throw over myself as I squatted in the bath. I had been used to taking showers. How could I sit in the bath? It was filthy to sit in your own bath water, wasn't it? How could people sit in dirty water?

The lady who owned the house, my landlady, was so amazed because she would hear me go to the bathroom in the morning and in the evening and she became concerned that I was bathing so often and she asked Trevor if I was all right because I was washing myself so much.

He told her, "Yes, it's because she comes from Trinidad that she bathes twice a day. That's what they do there."

At that time Trevor was living in Colindale and Eileen wasn't too far away from me.

The first doctor I had up here was Dr David Pitt, who was very politically active and later became a Lord: Lord Pitt of Hampstead. I knew him from the time I arrived as he was a friend of Trevor's. We would go to his home and of course to his surgery.

I really landed on my feet because everything was in place for me when I came. My first impression of England was that it was going to be great because I was met with open arms and everything was done to make me comfortable and to help me settle in.

Because Eileen, Trevor and the others I met seemed to be doing so well, I had hope for myself and was looking forward to starting my training to be a teacher.

At this stage I only saw Trevor as a platonic friend; there were no romantic stirrings at all on my side. He later confessed that he had ideas about me in his head. Apparently, he had 'liked' me since we were in school, but for me there was nothing there beyond friendship.

My landlady and her husband had two children and there was Marie, another lodger, who lived on the top floor. She was an editor at the *Daily Worker* a newspaper of communist party and there was another lodger called Rudy Daniel, who was also working for the Communist Party.

Nobody ever pushed any political views on me, not even Trevor. He never pushed communism on me all through his life. I did what I wanted and I was never coerced into anything. I became friends with his communist friends but they knew I wasn't part of their 'faith', so to speak. I had my own political views and that was that.

And, Trevor later said he would never tell me to stop dancing because he saw what happened when Clifford decided to try and control me. (Although, later on, Trevor did start criticising some aspects of my career).

Around the time of my arrival in the fifties, Trevor and most of his friends were involved in the student movement, which had a number of leading figures who would go on to become future prime ministers and other dignitaries.

It was a pretty dynamic bunch and they were very active in politics, social issues and African and Caribbean affairs. Around that time Richard Hart, the historian, lawyer and politician, was in that crowd, so was Cheddi Jagan, who later became the Prime Minister of Guyana, which was known as British Guiana.

And among them was a mature young lady called Claudia Jones, who was Trevor's cousin. She had gone to live in American from her birthplace in Belmont in Trinidad when she was just a little girl, but after becoming involved in communist politics in the USA she was rounded up by the government, put in prison, even though she was a sick woman, and afterwards she was deported to England.

She was supposed to have gone to Trinidad but the Governor of Trinidad had said he didn't want this communist woman in the country, so she ended up being sent to England.

Claudia came to England the same year as me, in 1955. I came in July and she arrived some time later in the year. She was someone who lived and breathed politics and she and Trevor would get involved in some heated political debates. That's when they were in their element. You were left in no doubt that they were intent on putting the world to rights. She had gained a lot of experience in the United States and Trevor and the others looked up to her as a real leader.

She was slightly older for a start and had been on the receiving end of the full force of American 'justice' for her radical political beliefs, so she was seen as tough and a no-nonsense sort of person.

None of them had experienced anything like the kind of things that she had been part of so she had a lot to teach Trevor and his comrades, but when they got into their arguments and political debates some of us would disappear upstairs and just leave them to it.

I was never that political and I found a lot of those discussions quite overbearing, although Claudia was a fun person to be around. For all her seriousness and sense of purpose, she still laughed a lot and was very outgoing, so I enjoyed her company.

Claudia suffered from tuberculosis and had heart problems, but she smoked like a chimney and she would never finish a cigarette. A lot of those fellows used to hang around her so they could get hold of her dog ends from the ashtray, because she would light a fag, take a few puffs and then put it in the ashtray before lighting another one and doing the same thing. Those guys would hoover up her leftover cigarettes and hang on her every word.

I used to go and press Claudia's hair. Back in the days before hair salons, we used to straighten hair with the hot comb, which you would heat up on the stove or kerosene lamp. We were very resourceful.

Claudia and I developed quite a friendship, although she was more like an aunt or older cousin to me and was very good at dispensing advice, especially about how we needed to concentrate on improving our skills and ambitions, and actually getting on with things rather than just talking about them.

In time, I found myself dancing in some of the activities that Claudia organised, like the first Caribbean carnivals and beauty pageants which she organised through her newspaper, *the West Indian Gazette,* which she edited.

The first carnival was held at St Pancras Town Hall in London, back in 1959, and that was extraordinary. We didn't go out on the streets; it was more like a lavish indoor gala with music, dancing and other performances.

The West Indian Gazette was one of the first black newspapers in England. If you were a black actor, writer, musician or a dancer, like I was, you could always count on that paper to give you some publicity.

I remember one of my first write-ups in her paper was for a play I did called *The Irregular Verb to Love* by Hugh and Margaret Williams, which Claudia came to review for her paper.

We had a Royal command performance that particular night, and after the show we all had to line up for the Queen, the Duke of Edinburgh, Princess Margaret and other dignitaries in the royal party. Her Majesty came by and we curtsied and nobody moved until the queen moved.

I remember Tony Armstrong-Jones, Princess Margaret's husband, made a beeline to come and talk to me. At that time he'd just come back from a holiday in Trinidad and wanted to talk to me about my country, so that was rather nice.

I don't think I knew about it at the time, but I think I later found out that Sparrow had done a calypso about Princess Margaret and 'de cameraman', that was what Tony Armstrong-Jones did: he was a photographer. I am glad that calypso didn't come up as a topic of conversation, otherwise I may have wanted the ground to open up and swallow me.

It was a good feeling to be performing for the royal family, although the whole cast found it a bit nerve-racking.

Claudia Jones was a bit magisterial, in her own way. She had people running behind her like she was some kind of Pied Piper and she could be a bit bossy and arrogant, but saying that, she was such a warm, open person and there were never any airs and graces about her.

She was a beautiful lady: lovely to look at, but she was also quite bold and would tell you off if she had to, but there was never anything daunting or aloof about her; she was very down to earth. Her health was very fragile, though, and there were times when she would just collapse with exhaustion.

It is interesting that we both came up to England in the same year. She was someone for me to hang on to in a way and I looked up to her like an aunt or an older cousin.

There was no denying that Claudia was someone for our community to respect and admire and I think she was one of the greatest leaders the black community in Britain has ever had.

Chapter Ten

Settling Down

About two or three days after I arrived in London I got a job as a clerk at an office near Mornington Crescent, in north London. It was at an office near where a mass murderer had lived, a grisly fact that I discovered some time later.

I remember that I took the train from Camden town and it went past Mornington Crescent, so I couldn't get off at that stop. I went back and tried again but the same thing happened. I tried a third time, and it happened yet again. In the end, I decided to walk to work because none of the trains seemed to be stopping at the station where I worked.

What I later discovered was that it was only the Charing Cross trains that used to stop at Mornington Crescent. The trains that went *via* Bank branched off elsewhere, so that every time I had got on the train it was going *via* Bank and therefore didn't stop at blooming Mornington Crescent!

Anyway, I sorted out my route and kept that job for a long time. After I left, I went to work as a darkroom technician at the London Hospital in Whitechapel in east London.

I was supervised there by a lovely Scottish lady who was head of the darkroom. She 'adopted' me and, apart from showing me 'the ropes' on the job, told me what to do and what not to do when I got married.

She used to say, "If you let him start a certain way you will have to put up with that bad habit all your life, so start as you mean to go on."

She was a real 'salt of the earth' type, and a fountain of home-grown wisdom and plain common sense.

She had a deep, deep Scottish accent and I couldn't understand half of what she said so I used to say 'yes' and 'no' and she would do the same to me, because, although I was speaking English, some people had trouble understanding my accent.

Around then, I decided I wanted to be a radiographer but I wouldn't have been able to do that job even if I wanted to because every so often they would take a blood test and that's when they discovered that I was anaemic.

I didn't know why until years later when the sickle cell trait was discovered. Back then, I was always anaemic and they used to give me iron tablets, but it meant that I wouldn't have been able to become a radiographer.

Never mind, I had still landed on my feet. I was working in a good job and had never had the experience of so many people who complained that they couldn't get rooms to rent or decent jobs to do because of racial prejudice. Those were the days when people would put up signs saying, 'No blacks, no dogs, no Irish' and, sometimes, 'no children'.

I often say I had it easy, and never had a problem wondering where my next meal was coming from or where my next job was coming from. I have been very lucky.

Eileen was working at County Hall at the London County Council (LCC), and Trevor was working at an optical firm in Poland Street in Soho, Central London. Trevor's friends had arranged for him to get that job, and in his spare time he was getting on with his studies because he really wanted to be an architect. That was what he had come to England to study, and he was determined to qualify and get work.

He was going to night school, a polytechnic on Regent's Street in Central London, along with his friends Alton and Ivan, who also had ambitions to become professionals. And Trevor was living in the house of his friend and mentor, Billy Strachan, who was much older and experienced, so provided a lot of support and grounding.

Billy had been an RAF pilot during the war. In the post-war period, in the fifties, he was very active in the Communist Party of Great Britain, and he was working at County Hall, home of the London County Council, where Eileen also had a job.

They all made sure that I was doing well and, in turn, whenever other people would arrive from Trinidad I would do my bit to help them get work at my workplace. It really was good, the way we helped each other. It was around that time that I first met the actress Carmen Munroe and we started going around together. I think that's why my life turned out to be in show-business because I met the 'showbiz people' before the teaching people. Boscoe Holder was already in England, and he was very involved in the performing arts, so I was building up my network of contacts.

Around that time, Oliver Messel, the uncle of Tony Armstrong-Jones (Princess Margaret's husband's), was commissioned to paint a Black Madonna and Boscoe recommended me as his muse.

In those days, the '50s and '60s, I didn't ask a lot of questions, I just did what I was asked to do. I sat for him and that's all I can remember, really.

Somewhere, there is a portrait of the Black Madonna modelled after me and painted by one of Britain's most celebrated artist and theatre designers. I haven't a clue where it is or how much it's worth.

I had known Trevor almost all my life; we'd grown up together as children in the same neighbourhood in Trinidad. As I said, on our first meeting, I had whacked him upside the head when I thought he was responsible for throwing a missile at me in class. It turned out to be mistaken identity. Another boy had thrown the offending object, but I was in no hurry to apologise to this young man who always had a way of sticking his head in the air as though he was superior to everyone around him.

I didn't come to England to live with Trevor, or anything like that – far from it. I had just left a relationship that had gone horribly wrong and I was in no hurry to get myself involved with anyone else.

I think I was over Clifford before I had left home. Not so much over him, I had just put him out of my mind. When I put something away, I lose all sensitivity to it, especially if it's something that has hurt me. As far as our relationship went, I knew there was no going back, although Clifford was writing to me and hoping for reconciliation. From my point of view, that was out of the question.

Before I'd left Trinidad, my aunt had taken me to some solicitors and taken out an affidavit that she would be responsible for my daughter, Dian-Marie. Clifford was always saying that he would take her but I made auntie swear that she would be responsible for her and wouldn't let him have her.

When I first came to England Trevor had a white girlfriend, like the majority of black guys who had white girlfriends or wives in those days. Despite that, Trevor always had this thing about promoting black people and black culture. He told me later that he was endeared to me because, apart from everything else, I was black.

When I came to England, he was in the Young Communist League because he was too young to be in the main party. He was very active, going off to sell the newspapers outside tube stations and wherever they were holding their meetings or rallies. About a week after I arrived, he went away to Warsaw on Communist Party business.

The communists had very interesting activities going on back then. Trevor and his associates were very good at combining politics and entertainment. I am sure I wouldn't have met some of the more fascinating and famous people I have met if it wasn't for their circle. I met people like Paul Robeson and lots of others through their network. Years later, after South Africa's independence, I met Nelson Mandela.

I can't really explain how Trevor and I got together but we got married about six months after I came up here. There wasn't really any organised courtship as such; no big love affair. He just proposed one day after suggesting that we should get married.

I wrote to my cousin Joyce in the United States asking her what I should do. She wrote back and said something like, "What are you waiting for? Girl, marry the man, no!"

What she said suddenly made me realise that I'd better think seriously about the proposal otherwise I would be on my own. It was a frightening prospect to be alone in a strange country.

I suppose it made sense to get married. I mean, he wasn't exactly a stranger or a new acquaintance. I knew him from home, we got on well, we knew each other's families and we had friends in common. On the whole, we had a lot going for us, I decided. Marrying just seemed like the logical thing to do. Consequently, Trevor always said that if it wasn't for Joyce I wouldn't have married him.

By that time I had quite a few friends, some of whom had recently come up from Trinidad: Alton, Vernon, Shirley and Ivan, who were all living in Paddington at the time and we used to get together to socialise.

Trevor and I actually got married on the last day of the year, December 31st, 1955. Bouge, a friend from Trinidad, was the best man and gave us away. Our other friends there were Alfred and Kathryn and my Auntie Maud, who had come up especially for the wedding and stayed with us for a while.

It was a small wedding and the church was just around the corner so we walked there and back. There was snow on the ground and it was just like a picture-postcard image of a white Christmas. The reception doubled up into an end-of-the-year and New Year's party with lots of food, good company and high spirits.

Anyway, a few months later, in February 1956, we moved to 53 Cromwell Avenue, in North London, which came up for rental. Ivan, Alton, Vernon, Shirley, Trevor and I moved in and split the rent. The property had about eight bedrooms, three kitchens, three living rooms and three toilets, but only one bathroom. It was one of those houses with three floors, and the rooms were huge.

We had all known each other from Trinidad and we'd practically grown up together from children and knew each other's families. We did everything together: the cooking, liming, going out to parties. People didn't like to invite us to their parties very much because a whole gang of us would turn up at their place.

Meanwhile, everybody knew our address because there was always something going on there. And, later, most of the people who came up from Trinidad, passed through that house. They came and stayed with us for a while, even if they just spent three or four days, until they had settled and found their own place. Often, we would even go and meet them at the station or the airport.

I like to say that we lived in one of the first communes in London. Trevor and I were the only two who were married initially, but we saw other marriages follow and they used to joke that Trevor was responsible for them getting married, as though he was some kind of matchmaker or marriage broker.

The house has since been divided into flats, but, would you believe that, 50 years later, it still has some of our original group living there?

I like communal living. In fact, I have never lived on my own in my entire life. I came from Trinidad living in a house that was full of people, and, throughout my life, that has been the pattern. It's what I'm used to and in many ways, it's what I need. When people talk about the privacy I can have on my own, I don't care. I like living with people.

Chapter Eleven

Fire Down Below

Michael X was one of the main characters creating a stir in London around that time in the late fifties and sixties. I knew him from Trinidad before he left for England in the fifties and changed his name from Michael de Freitas to Michael X, after the American civil rights activist Malcolm X.

Michael was working for Peter Rachman, a notorious landlord from West London who used to own a lot of houses, although many of them were really run-down and unfit for human habitation. He housed blacks and poor whites who couldn't get decent places to live anywhere else. People would be housed so many to a room and landlords like him would charge what was called the 'black tax', which were high rents that were way above the going rate for really poor quality housing.

Rachman was tough and vicious. He had no time for 'tea and sympathy' or hard-luck stories. If you didn't pay your rent, he would put you out on the streets in broad daylight. He evicted women and children with their bags and baggage. That was in the days before rent tribunals and that sort of thing.

Michael X used to go and collect Rachman's rent with his dogs and if people wouldn't pay up he wasn't afraid to set the dogs on them or to chuck them out of the property. He had a bad reputation for that as one of Rachman's henchmen or 'heavies' as they called them.

Then he became quite serious with politics and the Black Power Movement, so that was another side of his split personality. On the other hand, he was prosecuted and imprisoned for inciting racial hatred after saying something very outspoken about how white men should be killed for assaulting black women.

Aside from that madness, he was one of the people responsible for opening the Black House, which was a cultural centre in Holloway Road, north London. It was one of the first dedicated community centres in the country for black people, focusing on the arts.

The project was good thing for a lot of reasons, especially because it got the kids off the streets and gave them something constructive to do. They used to go there and do arts and learn about their culture and so on. It got a lot of them out of trouble and for that alone it had to be applauded.

When he and his associates set up the Black House that was a plus and there was hope that a lot of underprivileged people would benefit from it.

On the day they opened the Black House I performed some poems and I remember that John la Rose, the publisher and activist, made a presentation as well.

At that time, Michael X was moving with John Lennon from the pop group The Beatles and some of his celebrity set. The word was that Michael used to cut John's hair or act as his bodyguard or whatever, but he was well in with that fashionable crowd.

Of course, that connection put him in the limelight and in the gossip columns because John Lennon was one of the most famous musicians in the world, and his relationship with Yoko Ono was constantly in the news because they were always staging different publicity stunts for world peace.

You know, we Trinidadians always used to say that Michael wasn't all that hot, but, somehow, he managed to land on his feet. He always gave the impression that he was some kind of big shot and had a lot of people in awe of him because of all his Black Power chat, but I honestly don't think he was all that respected.

There was a whole set of confusion with that man. He was a bit arrogant. He felt he could do whatever he liked but he took things a bit far and it all got out of hand. The Black House ran out of money and was struggling along until it burned down in mysterious circumstances.

Michael made big news when he was involved in allegations about a serious crime: extortion. The authorities knew very well that he was going to skip bail but they granted bail anyway, and sure enough, he absconded.

They say he stowed away on a boat and went back to Trinidad, which is ironic since you often heard about people stowing away to go to England. When he got to Trinidad, he ended up in even more trouble when his cousin and a young English woman who was moving around with him, were killed.

Eventually, the government hanged him. He had put a little island like Trinidad in the news all over the world for all the wrong reasons.

Edmundo Rosso was another Trinidadian but, unlike Michael X, he was making a good name for himself in England with his rumba band. When he went to the UK he adopted a kind of showbiz persona and said he was Venezuelan.

It was easy for him to say that because there's only about 20 miles between the two countries anyway, and I suppose it's more exotic to say you're Venezuelan than Trinidadian. And, his complexion gave it some credibility, I suppose.

There was a phrase that some white people used a lot in the old days to describe light-skinned black people. They said they were 'easier on the eye'. They thought light-skinned people were more attractive than those with darker complexions. Unfortunately, many black people fell into the trap of believing that rubbish as well.

That idea was something that I came across a lot later on when I started working in television. You would find people being cast for parts because of their skin tones and not for what they could really do.

Those things really upset me and sometimes I expressed my displeasure. I am sure there were times when I probably talked too much and get myself out of favour.

Trinidad is a country made up of people from across the spectrum of the rainbow, so I grew up with all types of different people and we always believed in merit. That was the main thing, not who you knew or what shade you were.

Anyway, that business about some people being 'easier on the eye' was a fact of life in Britain, and it's something we had to get used to, although it was done in a very underhand way. When I started performing here I used to dance with a lot of the people who came up from Trinidad to do shows. Of course, I knew most of them already from home, so whenever a production came here that called for dancers, then I would be called up and given a part.

In 1957, a couple of years after we were married, Trevor got called up to do his National Service, but he absconded and went to Moscow. Before he left, I got a job at a company called Contemporary Films in central London, which was a left-wing, independent film production company. It was run by a group of socialists who used to do films that would be shown in independent cinemas.

That experience taught me that it's never good to tell a lie, because it will always come back to haunt you.

I was doing clerical work there and one day I got chosen to do some dancing in a new film that was being made by a different company. The stars were Robert Mitchum and Rita Hayworth, Hollywood celebrities, and the film was called *Fire Down Below (1957)*, which was based on the Nobel-prize winning book by William Golding.

Those lead actors were household names and it was a big Hollywood production. Filming had already started in Trinidad and for the England end of the shoot they brought up some limbo dancers and musicians from the island, but they needed some extras and I managed to get taken on as one of the dancers. That was to be my first 'serious' role as a performer in this country. To think, I was going to be in a film, my first motion picture! I couldn't wait, even though I was just an extra.

The opportunity to do the film sounded very exciting, so I decided to moonlight. I didn't go to work on the day of the shoot, I called in sick and told them I had laryngitis. This was what, years later, the English now famously call "pulling a sickie!", that is telling lies about being sick to get out of going to work.

So, when the day arrived, I left home earlier than usual and, instead of going to the office, I went to the film set. We were on call from five o'clock in the morning and on the first take of the first scene of the day, I caught fire – literally.

I was part of a group of dancers who were supposed to be going along in a solemn procession. We had to carry lighted sparklers as we swayed or danced along in the parade.

I was wearing a Spanish-style outfit with a mantilla and, unfortunately, the person behind me touched my outfit with her sparkler and, suddenly, the headdress ignited and went up in flames.

Clary Whales, who was playing the piano, and Edric Connor, one of our leading Trinidadian actors, who were both on set, noticed what had happened and the two of them were shouting out, "Roll de girl...roll de girl!", indicating that they should roll me on the floor but no-one came near me because I was on fire and, naturally I suppose, everyone kept their distance and screamed or scarpered out of the way.

Suddenly, I registered what Edric was saying and, quick as a flash, I shot down on the floor and rolled myself along the ground to try and put out the flames.

There was such a commotion as everyone ran around trying to help me, and eventually someone must have arrived with a bucket of water — by which time the worse was over. They called an ambulance and when that arrived they put me on a stretcher and took me to hospital. I was admitted and kept in there for about six weeks.

I lost all my hair and I had third degree burns down my neck and all down my arms. I still have the marks on my upper body. I remember getting a lot of injections, which were painkillers they were using to tackle the pain.

I think I was the first patient at that hospital in Barnet who they treated for burns by not treating the actual burns. Instead, they just put me on a drip and gave me those injections. There were no ointments or creams to heal the burns; they were just left to heal by themselves. The technique proved successful.

I had to try not to touch the skin but it was so painful and it used to itch so much. All I could do to get some relief was to pat my burns until they crusted over.

Interestingly, the day I got injured was Princess Margaret's birthday, and I think the story of me catching fire knocked her off the front page of at least one of the newspapers.

One paper announced, 'Fire Down Below Girl Caught Fire on Top', something like that, and there was only a small headline in the Evening News about Princess Margaret. Some of those papers went to Trinidad and a number of people there thought that I had actually died as a result of that accident.

What a fix I was in! I had caught fire while Trevor was away. I had lied to my workplace and told them I was off sick yet they saw the truth in the evening news and the morning papers the very next day. And now I was in hospital for over a month in terrible pain, feeling sorry for myself.

Trevor came back as soon as he heard about my predicament, but he was still trying to get out of doing National Service. Every time the door bell rang he jumped up in fear because he thought they had come for him. In those days they used to come physically and take you away if you didn't respond to the correspondence, and they used to put people in prison for not doing their civic duty by completing the National Service.

Because he was in the Communist Party, Trevor didn't believe in the National Service scheme and so he used his contacts to get him away to Moscow. From there, he travelled to Poland and various other places. He never did do that two year National Service; he managed to evade the authorities on that one.

I had done my bit of evading too, because I never plucked up the courage to face my bosses and colleagues at Contemporary Films. I was too ashamed.

After all, I had told them that I was sick and couldn't go in to work. The truth was that I was off moonlighting on a film set. Some people would say it served me right: I had called for sickness and it came with a vengeance.

Chapter Twelve

Cleopatra

The late fifties and sixties were my heyday: I had so many opportunities to dance. Just about everything going that called for a black dancer had me in it. I was very lucky and, more often than not, I was in the right place at the right time.

I used to dance with a lot of the people who came up from Trinidad to do shows. They would just rope me in and most of the time that was a lot of fun.

Because of how I had been burnt in the film *Fire Down Below*, I joined the actors' union, Equity. Edric Connor, a friend of ours and one of the leading black actors around at the time advised me to join and arranged for me to get in, so I did and have been with Equity since 1957.

I got compensation for the accident and that money provided a down payment when we bought us our first house and moved from the shared property we called 'the commune'. It was at that house that we had our son, Mick. But, before that, practically as soon as we moved in, I did my first tour as a dancer in the UK when a group of us went to Spain for about a month.

It came about after I had started doing some television work on a programme called *Cool for Cats (1956-1961)*, which was a show promoting all the latest pop groups. It featured the new singles, the latest dance moves and interviews with the new and emerging stars, and was a sort of fore-runner to *Top of the Pops*, which came later on the BBC.

I was one of the girls on *Cool for Cats* who danced to the songs or posed around in different costumes.

While I was working on the show, which was made by Rediffusion, I had an encounter one day that really put a spring in my step. I was walking down the corridor of the studio when I saw this tall, handsome, dreamy-looking black man coming towards me. I might even have thought about pinching myself because such visions were rare, to say the least.

In fact, it was a vision, yes, none other than Marvin Gaye, who was in the country to promote one of his records for *Tamla Motown* and making an appearance on *Cool for Cats*.

I couldn't believe my eyes but I was determined not to stare, so I looked away and tried to make myself invisible because I'm not the kind of person to go up to famous people and make a big fuss.

Well, he made a beeline for me and came up to speak to me, didn't he? I suppose he did that as one black person to another, especially as it was rare to see more than one of us in one place at that time.

I was elated. Don't ask me what we talked about, but my head was in the clouds for weeks after that and I hardly wanted to wash my hand after he had shaken it. I was just like a typical fan who got to meet one of her heroes, but who could blame me?

Marvin Gaye was not only very, very talented but he was certainly one of the most handsome men I had ever seen. In the flesh, he looked every bit as good as he did on the TV, so that was certainly my lucky day.

Working on *Cool for Cats* was a lot of fun and full of surprises like that. I have to thank Joan Kemp-Welch for giving me the chance to work on the show and for letting me stay on until I was seven and a half months pregnant with my son Mick. By then, I wasn't exactly jiving like the rest of the other girls, but Joan would put me in fancy chairs or on loungers just posing to the music, so that was pretty easy-going until I left to have my baby.

Joan was an amazing person. I think she was one of the first women directors working in TV at that time, so she was a pioneer. I understand that she died in 1999, although I had lost contact with her since she gave me that break on TV all those years ago.

I did *Cool for Cats* regularly because it was weekly show and then after I left and just before I had the baby, Buddy Bradley, an

American choreographer, decided to get a dance group together to do a tour of Spain.

He took me, Raymond McClean, a dancer from Trinidad with whom I had danced before leaving the island, Margaret Freeman, a dancer from Cardiff, and Freddie Keeting, a mixed-race dancer, also from Cardiff.

The tour of Spain with Buddy took place in 1958. It started to feel as though I was picking up from where I had left off in Trinidad when I was doing all that dancing and touring around.

On that trip I performed with Raymond McClean, but from then on everywhere I went to do shows I was with Eveard Puckering, whom I danced with for years. We were quite a team and organised our own tour of Europe in the years that followed.

Puckering and I called ourselves *The Primitives* and we travelled all over Europe and even went to Japan, doing our 'exotic' and 'traditional' Caribbean dances. I don't think there was an American military base in Europe that we didn't perform at.

The other person I went abroad with after Buddy was Edmundo and his band. There were three dancers from Trinidad, including myself, on that tour.

We used to do the limbo, which was a very popular dance in the clubs where we performed. It was a Caribbean dance where you had to bend over backwards and dance under a pole held up at different heights – or should I say different 'lows' – because the lower it got the more agile and flexible you had to be to get underneath it.

We used to do other dances but that one was really the speciality in those days. That's when I met a dancer called Della McKenzie, who was famous for doing the limbo.

Around that time I also worked with Cy Grant, who was getting a lot of acting work and was also a calypsonian. He was one of the few black people on television in those days and had a part in a BBC current affairs show called *Tonight*, where he used to sing calypsoes about events that had happened in the day's news.

I also worked with Nadia Catouse and Edric Connor, who were the leading black performers of the day, along with Earl Cameron, who was my favourite black actor. I danced in the film *Flame in the Streets (1961)*, which Earl starred in along with John Mills and Sylvia Syms.

Flame in the Streets was an important film that dealt with racial tensions and prejudice. It was about a trade union leader who fights for the rights of his black workers but who faces conflict at home when his own daughter decides to marry a West Indian. That filmed opened a whole can of worms and was a big talking point.

I was also a dancer in the film *Cleopatra (1963)* with Richard Burton, Elizabeth Taylor and Rex Harrison. They say that was the film that nearly bankrupted the studio, Twentieth Century Fox. It cost over $40million, which was an absolute fortune in those days.

Well, it is still a lot of money today, although nowadays they think nothing of spending over a hundred million on a Hollywood movie. In those days, that kind of budget was outrageous and apparently it didn't make back the money at the box office, so in that sense it was supposed to have been a flop.

Liz Taylor's fee alone was £1million pounds, which was unheard of for an actress in those days, and filming was moved from the US to Rome, which entailed all manner of hitches and glitches.

We dancers, who were extras, never really came into contact with the big stars very much. They were the biggest celebrities around in those days and they were real superstars, who were considered almost super-human, and the way they were treated was out of this world. Also, the newspapers were full of gossip about Elizabeth and Richard's love life, which was reputedly as hot and fiery as her infamous bad temper.

I remember that Liz Taylor was a very tiny woman of about four foot nine or something like that. She would come in looking very ordinary, so plain in fact that she wouldn't turn any heads but by the time they spent hours with her in make-up she would come out looking like a million dollars, no kidding. She really was stunning to look at after that transformation. And her eyes were magical: she had the most beautiful blue eyes I have ever seen in my life; they were mesmerising. To me they were blue but I have heard people describing them as violet.

She was a chain smoker and always used to be puffing away on her cigarettes, and she was constantly getting fussed over by all the directors and the assistants on the set. That was to be expected, really, as she was Hollywood royalty and treated just like the queen bee is expected to be, and was always the centre of attention.

At the time, I didn't think anything strange about the fact that Elizabeth Taylor was cast to play Cleopatra because the story was about a beautiful and powerful woman who ruled a land called Egypt and to them that called for a beautiful and powerful woman to play the part. And, I suppose, the most beautiful woman of the day was considered to be Elizabeth Taylor, so there you are.

It would take someone like Claudia Jones in the 1950s to organise the black beauty pageants in England before people started waking up to our own images of beauty: the idea that black women were beautiful.

Before that, the beauty pageants that were held did not consider us capable of entering because we didn't have the ivory skin and the angular noses and other features that they called beautiful.

Another thing, the way black history is taught now, we get more of an idea of what the world was really like, so people will know that the Ancient Egyptians were black and that they built the pyramids and had that civilization. But, as far as Hollywood was concerned, there was nothing odd or strange about casting a white woman to play the part of an Egyptian queen called Cleopatra.

It was just the same way that Tarzan was the king of the jungle, and he was a white man. Incidentally, I was also an extra, dancing in a Tarzan film or two. Those were the films being made that had parts for black people; we couldn't really pick and choose because those sorts of roles were the only ones available.

How I got the part to dance in *Cleopatra* is a story in itself. They were looking for dancers who were at least five to five feet tall but, although I was shorter than the maximum height specified, I decided to go along to the audition. They measured us and I sucked in my breath and stretched myself up as far as I could but it was no good. I wasn't the right height and thought there was no way I'd get a call back. I just went off and thought nothing more about it.

About a week later the phone rang and a voice said, "Corinne Skinner, we're pleased to tell you that you've got the part in Cleopatra. We'll need you to come down to the office to…"

And I just said, "Yea, yea, pull the other one."

And the person on the phone said, "I beg your pardon?"

I thought it was a friend of mine joking around, so, I said, "Yea, yea, very funny joke. I got the part in Cleopatra? Pull the other one."

The person said, "Corinne Skinner I am calling from the casting director's office. Do you want the part or not?"

Well, I suddenly realised that it was serious. It was so embarrassing. I thought that since I'd failed the height test that there was no way I would be cast for the film.

They explained that, although I was a little shorter than they wanted, I was slim and had long legs, so it gave the illusion that I was actually quite tall, and that had nailed it. I got my first contract for six weeks to go off and film in Rome and that ran into months.

I must have been away for over six months; the contract just kept rolling on and on. However, in the finished film, the sequence I am in probably lasted about sixty seconds if that much.

More dancing roles for film and television came along around that time. I did a film called *Call Me Bwana (1963)*, which starred Bob Hope.

One particular day, while we were shooting, it became very foggy and there were a lot of delays because of the weather. By evening, when it was time for us to go home, Bob Hope made such a fuss because he wanted us to stay on and work a bit longer. He kept referring to us as, 'you people' and complained because we were due to wrap for the day and he wanted us to carry on working, although there were equity rules about that.

It was horrible because you started seeing another side of this world-famous Hollywood 'star' who was such a popular comedian and everyone thought he was such a nice guy in real life. His true colours were coming out and it was a bit off.

Things were difficult enough with the fog, it had been a long day with an early call time as always when we were filming, but, he kept insisting we had to carry on and was getting more and more bad-tempered. I am not sure what he was used to back in the States but our representatives were sticking to their guns and insisting that if we were going to work overtime it had to be negotiated and paid for, stuff like that. I think we may have gone on strike if he had carried on but the directors stepped in and let us go.

As soon as anybody says, 'you people' it gets my back up because it's just rude. Who the hell did he think he was? I didn't like him very much after that experience.

I was a belly dancer in *A Funny Thing Happened on the Way to the Forum (1966)* starring Frankie Howerd. And there was some more 'exotic dancing' in something called *Arabian Nights* on the BBC.

In the early 1970s there was a chance to appear in the James Bond film, *Live and Let Die (1973)*, with Roger Moore in the lead role and my old friend and former teacher, Geoffrey Holder, doing choreography.

Geoffrey also had a leading role in the film, which was exciting to do, especially as most of us doing the dancing already knew one another.

The film was set on a Caribbean island and we were in our element. I played a young woman who was being sacrificed in a voodoo scene and the dance sequence involved me flailing about as they carried me off to be sacrificed to the voodoo gods. It was a lot of fun, but let's just say I don't think either of my grandmothers would have approved.

Now, Geoffrey was a real character. As I said before, this man is about six foot six or seven tall. He's a big, strapping bloke, and in the film he played a menacing character who is obviously in charge: ruling over everyone using voodoo and fear.

However, in one scene towards the end of the film, he had to fall into a coffin full of snakes. Just one problem with that – Geoffrey had a phobia of snakes. The man was petrified of snakes; absolutely petrified.

During rehearsals they got the stand-in guy to do the run-through and on every occasion that he did the scene, Geoffrey, who was watching from the sidelines, would let out a loud noise as the man fell into the coffin. Geoffrey's sound effects were so off-putting but, anyway, that was his thing as he got into character.

Well, the time came for him to do a take and Geoffrey did the scene by rushing into the coffin full of snakes and bouncing up like a jack-in-the-box. Then, quick as a flash, he rushed back to the dressing room.

The really funny thing was that there weren't real snakes in the coffin, they were all plastic. They only used real ones for the close ups. Still, real or not, Geoffrey wasn't sticking around to find out. He rushed through the scene like a manic and then went and took refuge in his dressing room. It was just so funny to think of this big, larger-than-life man being afraid of anything, much less some plastic snakes.

Anyway, there was a not-so-funny upshot because the guy who was the snake handler on the set actually got bitten by one of his snakes, so Geoffrey probably took that as justification for his phobia.

It was after doing productions like *Live and Let Die* that I decided I'd had enough of the dancing and wanted to have a go at acting.

When I stopped dancing it was because I had danced in every place that there were opportunities and in every film and television show that called for black dancers. So, I said, OK, I'm finished with dancing.

Everyone said, "But why?"

They thought I was doing really well and couldn't understand my decision.

I stopped dancing when I was on top. I told them: "I'm stopping while people are still asking for me to dance and I'm not going to wait until my belly gets too big and I'm decrepit and people say 'Oh gosh, why that Corinne Skinner don't stop dancing?'"

I wasn't going to do that, I wanted to quit while I was ahead.

And I never danced again after that, but, would you believe that a lot of people never even knew that I'd ever been a dancer? I stopped it altogether and I started doing private acting lessons with a drama tutor called Wendy Wisby.

I used to turn up for auditions for acting roles and directors would say, "Oh, Corinne, you're such a good dancer, why do you want to do acting?"

As I would say, "I don't dance anymore; I'm acting now."

When you go for one thing and they picture you in the role that they had always seen you in, then they can't imagine you doing anything else. However, I was adamant that I was no longer going to dance and that's how it was.

Then I had a little part in a TV play called *In the Beautiful Caribbean (1972)* by Barry Reckord. Louise Bennett, popularly known as 'Miss Lou', a wonderful Jamaican poet and actress, was in it. She came over especially to do the play and we became good friends.

During one of our conversations I told her that I liked grapefruits and do you know that after the play finished and she went back to Jamaica, I was at home one day and an express van pulled up outside my house with a delivery for me. Louise had sent me a whole box of grapefruits from Jamaica. I think they came off her land where she had all kinds of fruit trees. Now, that was some gesture.

It was around that time that I started telling my colleagues how difficult I was finding it to do acting because casting directors and producers kept talking to me about dancing, which is precisely what I didn't want to do. My friend Joan Ann Maynard said to me, "Why don't you go and do a teacher training course that also gives you the chance to do drama?"

It wasn't exactly what I wanted to do, so I said I'd think about it. Then, I did another play at the Institute of Contemporary Arts (ICA), with Anton Phillips, Horace James and Joan Ann Maynard, and she asked me again about doing the teaching.

Anton, Horace and Joan Ann were already doing teaching and keeping their hand in with the acting whenever they could get parts.

In the end, Joan Ann took it upon herself to get prospectuses from different colleges and sent them to my home. Then, she rang me up and said, "Have you applied for any courses yet?"

Deciding I had nothing to lose, I applied to Trent Park teacher training institute and the Rose Bruford Theatre College, and I got into Trent Park. That's where I did a course in teacher training combined with the performing arts.

I majored in teaching junior school and that's how I ended up becoming a qualified teacher. By now, 18 years or so had passed since this timid young lady had arrived from Trinidad with the idea that she was going to fulfill her ambition to study and become a teacher.

In the meantime, I had been waylaid in the most remarkable way by a career in show-business which took me to some wonderful places around the world and to meetings with amazing people that I never imagined I would have met.

Now, a fresh opportunity and a new career beckoned but little did I know that the show-business bug had not quite finished with me yet.

Chapter Thirteen

Trevor

When we bought our first house at Glebe Road, in north London, Trevor said, "I'm buying this house and anybody who comes from Trinidad is welcome to stay here until they find their feet." That was always his motivation: to be able to help his country men in any way he could.

Around that time, I was doing more and more dancing and Trevor would come to see the shows. I think by then he'd moved on from wanting to be an architect. That's what he came to England to study, but somewhere along the line that ambition got thrown out so badly that I don't even think he remembered he had left Trinidad to study architecture. Once we saw how that profession was going in the UK and how limited opportunities were, we sat down and talked about it and he changed his mind and decided he wanted to go into education.

I think that the way his mind was working and how he was developing his ideas he drew the conclusion that architecture would have held him back, whereas he thought he could dovetail his interest in education with his love of politics. By that time he was getting more and more involved in politics, anyway, so it seemed a logical direction to take.

When he came back from Eastern Europe, after he thought the fuss about the National Service had blown over, he then went off to British Guiana (Guyana) to work with Cheddi Jagan, the young socialist leader. It was coming up to election time and Cheddi, who was head of his party, was pushing for leadership of the country. Trevor taught in one of the special technical schools over there and he was away from us for three years.

The children and I were due to go over there. Tickets were booked and bags packed, but just as we were going to leave Trevor got in touch and said, "I don't think you all should come here because it's getting too volatile with the politics and everything."

Unfortunately for him, Claudia Jones, his cousin, and our very special friend, died in December 1964 while he was still in British Guiana. That really shook him up. Trevor would have done anything to have had Claudia around. The two of them used to argue so much over politics and their discussions sounded like Parliamentary debates. I used to think they were going to fight the way they would argue and get heated up during a discussion. They were both communists and had a lot in common but when they clashed, boy, you would think they were going to war.

I don't think Trevor was ever surprised at how Claudia had emerged as a leader in British society. He used to hear reports about her in the USA but until she came here when she was deported from the States in 1955, he hadn't met her. He didn't know her personally up to then, although they were related. But, she came with a certain kind of stature, so all these people here rallied around her like drones around the queen bee.

I think Trevor was one of them and he was rather proud of who she was and what she'd gone through in the States because of her political beliefs. She was actually imprisoned for her ideas. For a communist, that was a badge of honour, so he had a tremendous amount of admiration for her. He was encouraged by her achievements over there and impressed by what she managed to achieve over here, also.

Claudia demonstrated that she had a lot of experience that he didn't have, and he was optimistic that some of her experience and charisma would rub off on him. She was clearly going places. I think she was one of the people who encouraged him to go to British Guiana and dedicate his skills to the independence movement there, which was one of the best and most rewarding things he ever did.

Trevor also used to have big political debates with a cousin of his called Jean George. I think she used to come round to our house just to have a fight with him over politics!

Well, the way he was could be quite infuriating. Once he started on something he never gave you a chance to talk and he was headstrong (and so were Claudia and Jean), so, they used to clash, but he wouldn't have had it any other way. It tickled me that these women were giving the men as good as they got, if not more.

Billy Strachan was Trevor's mentor. He had been seriously injured in the war and his hip was damaged so he had a little bubble car that could take just him, no passengers.

Whatever Billy said, Trevor and his associates would go with it. Sometimes I used to tell Trevor to get a life because his preoccupation was always following whatever Billy said. He even wanted to name any son we might have 'Billy' or 'Cheddi', after Cheddi Jagan. I told him, "over my dead body!"

My daughter Dian-Marie came up from Trinidad with her aunt Lorna and Trevor adopted her. When our second child was born, we named him Michel, not Billy or Cheddi, as Trevor intended, although Billy Strachan did become his godfather.

I had a friend in Trinidad called Michel and I'd always liked that name but people kept saying, "You can't call him Michel because that is a girl's name." Anyway, I insisted that Michelle is a girl's name, whereas the boy's name is different and is spelt M-i-c-h-e-l.

I might have been influenced by my mother who had given me a French name and also by my grandmother, who was from a French colony.

As a child, I knew somehow that when I had children I was going to give them French names. Yet all the people who knew us from the time our son was little called him 'Mick' and not Michel. All the people who met him when he was older, especially his basketball friends, called him Courtney.

Billy Strachan later went on to become a judge, and was a very good godfather to our boy. Every Christmas Eve night he used to come to see his godson and bring his present. And, of course, we prepared his favourite seasonal sweetbread and ham and he'd have his Christmas drink with us before he left.

When Trevor gave up his studies in architecture and started at teacher's training college, some friends of ours, Elfid and Karen, also went to the same college and ended up teaching in Nigeria.

Fortunately for Trevor, he had done his 'A' levels so he had the necessary exams to get him into the college and after that he went and taught in a secondary school.

He became Chairman of the Education Committee of the Race Equality Council in Hackney, East London, and Chair of the Caribbean Teachers' Association, which he co-founded along with people like Geoff Crawford.

Trevor was very happy being a teacher, more so than doing anything else.

This was back in the 1980s. We were quite a nice little family with Trevor doing his teaching, me doing some teacher training and bits of acting.

When people used to visit they would talk to Mick and Dian-Marie about my appearances on TV and say things like, "I never knew that was your mother on the television, why didn't you tell us?"

And Dian-Marie would say, "What is there to tell?"

The children just grew up used to it and never made any kind of fuss.

I was a restless parent because I was always up at Dian-Marie's school. I would just pop in to see the teachers and have a good chat about what they and the children were doing.

The kids would see me coming and would say, "Dian-Marie, your mum's coming, what did you do?"

But I wasn't there to complain, I was just there to see how they were getting on and what the school children were up to.

Dian-Marie knew she hadn't done anything wrong. She wasn't the type to get into trouble, but that unexpected visit by her mum kept her and her brother on their toes because I could go up there any old time, for no reason at all. I would just show up.

I was probably the only parent who did that. Although it was a very unconventional thing to do, Miss Jordan, the headmistress, was very understanding and, looking back on it now, she must have thought me a little bit eccentric, who knows?

Trevor and I were involved in the carnival in the UK since it started in the 1950s with Claudia Jones. The first carnival was held at St Pancras Town Hall in the winter, and it almost certainly coincided with the timing of the Trinidad carnival.

Obviously we had the cold weather while the people in Trinidad had the sunshine, and we were indoors while they had the freedom of the streets.

Some people actually turned up at the event in costume, which must have met with some funny stares when they were travelling on public transport. Mind you, if they were brave enough to have worn a carnival costume in the first place, I doubt if some funny looks from passers-by would have mattered much to them. In those days black people were used to be stared at just because the colour of our skin was different.

I was fortunate enough to have been involved in that first carnival because I was related to Claudia through my husband and also because I was a dancer who jumped at the chance to perform in the event. The dancers performed a floor show and did some folk dancing.

Around that same time Claudia also had her newspaper, *The West Indian Gazette*, and myself and a number of others would always be called on to do photo shoots for the paper. These were used in advertising or for editorial stories or whatever. I also did a lot of cabarets around that time, and people like Cy Grant, Nadia Catouse and other West Indians were also moving in that circuit.

After that first carnival, in the years following, the London carnival would be timed to take place around the same time as the event in Trinidad, but, apart from the feeling of high spirits there was very little real comparison, except that Claudia was very enterprising and she brought up celebrated calypsonians from Trinidad to perform in London.

I remember on one occasion after the carnival we all boarded a coach and went off to Manchester to perform in a night club owned by Lord Kitchener, who was the leading Calypsonian of the day. It was a fantastic event. I remember we danced the limbo.

Sparrow, who was then an emerging Calypsonian, and not yet fully world famous, travelled up with us because he had been over to take part in the carnival in London. There were other well-known names like the actor Horace James and Pat Castagne, who was a celebrated radio announcer from Trinidad. Although he was born in Guyana and moved to Trinidad when he was young, as far as we were concerned he was one of us.

Lord Kitch, as we called Lord Kitchener, was a born showman, as I have already indicated. He was from Arima in Trinidad and began performing quite young as a naturally gifted entertainer before becoming one of Trinidad's best-loved Calypsonians. He came to England on the Empire Windrush in 1948, along with Lord Beginner, another well-known performer, and made quite an impression on the entertainment circuit.

Whereas in the Caribbean we had carnivals and festivals of one kind or another, in England they tended to have fetes, the most famous of which were the annual Easter Parade and the Lord Mayor's Show.

The boroughs would put on a show about once a year in which businesses and utilities would parade in the street on floats before ending up in the town hall where the mayor would make a speech and give out awards.

As it happens, I used to do quite a few of these town hall events and several times I represented the Electricity Board. You can guess where this is coming from: other floats would represent gas, water, the building industry, and so forth.

I had to wear a costume of some kind, with a headdress, perhaps a light organza top and a frilly skirt and stockings and sandals. This was the 1950s and usually I was the only black person on a float, although later on they became more multi-racial, depending on which borough was organising a show.

It was at one of these events held in Kensington that they asked Russell Henderson, a pioneer of pan in this country, to take part with his combo. They were featured on a float and, of course, they made sure the news spread among their friends and families like wild fire and, sure enough, a big crowd turned out to support the event. As they came along, the crowd followed the float, dancing behind it as they played some lively calypsoes, just as though they were 'at home' in Trinidad.

It was a big thing at the time, and apparently the first time that a band had performed on a float, on the road in England. This was the 1950s when everything was much more starchy and conservative. That kind of excitement was usually confined to the nightclubs, so you can just imagine what an eye-opener that that was for the English folks and for the West Indians too, who started to get the flavour of 'home from home' at last.

Much later, the carnival came out on the streets of Notting Hill, although by then Claudia Jones was dead.

The Notting Hill Carnival began to get bigger and more daring. People would go to see who was actually brave enough to turn up in costume. By then the event was being held around August and it had become an independent entity, not a tag-on to one of the town hall fetes or utility exhibitions.

In around 1972 there was a big function at the Commonwealth Institute called the 'Mas in May'. In Trinidad around about the same time they had an outbreak of yellow fever and another epidemic, so carnival was postponed until the May of that year, several months later than usual.

While that was going on, people in England had the idea to try and do something at the Commonwealth Institute, I think to raise funds for Trinidad to help out with the damage caused by the epidemic. Hundreds of people performed. There was dancing, acting, skits, floor shows, beauty pageants, and so on.

Peter Minshall, an award-winning costume designer, designed the costumes for the entire programme, and Stanley Jack, a leading choreographer, who was responsible for choreographing virtually all of the carnival floor shows in the early days, did the choreography. I did two or three dances.

Later on that same year the Notting Hill Carnival came along and Peter's costumes were featured in the carnival, the first time professionally-designed costumes were worn at the carnival. It was spectacular. The bands then were quite small, with only about 20 or 30 people. Now they're more like 200-member bands.

The local councils around Notting Hill, Kensington and Chelsea, started getting interested in carnival and the local government body, the GLC — Greater London Council — decided to fund part of the carnival. For example, the education authority would give people money to go into schools and teach carnival arts.

Trevor was a leading officer with the Inner London Education Authority (ILEA), which had a very positive attitude towards multi-cultural and multi-racial education and that was very progressive.

I used to go into about four or five schools in the Notting Hill area to teach movement and about the history of carnival in the Caribbean.

In Trinidad, we don't just put on carnival for people to jump up in the street and carry on wantonly. It's about history and culture, so people learn what is behind the theme they are featuring. If they have a nautical theme, they learn to move like a sailor, not just gyrate but really learn the art of the thing, the history of sea-faring, as well as the historical and cultural contexts of the story they are telling.

It was very competitive and I became a judge selecting the best carnival costumes and bands. I still judge today, so that's been over forty years.

Over the years, more and more people started flocking to Notting Hill, some out of curiosity to begin with, others to let down their hair and get on bad. So, Notting Hill carnival has become the biggest street festival in Europe. Now, it is too crowded out and the atmosphere isn't the same as in the early days.

What I like about it here, though, is that they are interested in keeping the tradition of storytelling going, whereas in some places carnival is just a 'jump up' and the excuse for some uncontrolled behaviour with people turning up in their bikinis and not much left to the imagination.

The best bands to watch are the ones who can tell their story well through their performance. As a judge, I am looking for that polished appearance and performance and it's something I have been doing since the 1970s, so I guess I know what makes a good performance by now.

The first thing you look for is the visual impact of the band, especially as they enter the judging zone. Then you judge how well they display and carry off their costume; how they line up and present themselves as a team; how good their act is because, remember, they're telling a story; how well do they present that story and carry off their theme?

In the UK there has been a lot of talk about taking the carnival off the streets and holding it in London's Hyde Park, but I hate the idea of that.

It would be a big mistake to take the carnival down that road. Carnival needs to be free, on the street; it is all about freedom and abandonment, so it should not be contained in a confined space.

We might even end up with something resembling the West Indian carnival in New York, where they just parade down the boulevard and then end up in one place, just very contained and controlled. I am very old-fashioned and don't like the idea of carnival being taken away from the people.

Trevor was just the same and had the same opinion as me on this issue. Carnival is our thing; it's our expression and that's how it should remain.

Chapter Fourteen

Empire Road

I had just begun to work as a teacher at a school in east London when the call came for me to an episode of *Coronation Street*, which was then the biggest show on British television, watched by 18 million people or more.

The soap opera, set in Manchester, in the north of England, had been going since 1960 and had a huge fan base. It was everything that good dramas required: strong storylines, engaging and controversial characters, brilliant writing and lots of comedy and tragedy.

It went out once or twice a week and was (and still is) an iconic show with one of the most recognisable theme tunes in British television history.

What was especially good about it from the beginning was the fact that the show had strong women characters with names like Elsie Tanner, Rita Fairclough, Bet Lynch and Ena Sharples.

So, when I got the call to act in *Coronation Street* I was very excited, especially because that was my favourite TV show — and it still is.

I was cast to play a nurse who was looking after one of the lead characters called Stan Ogden, who was in hospital. Stan was famously married to the Street's battleaxe, Hilda Ogden, who permanently wore hair curlers and a hairnet and enjoyed 'supping' milk stout in the Rover's Return pub.

Stan was a big man who loved his 'grub' (food) and was always trying to get out of doing an honest day's work. In our scene, he had never been in hospital before and was quite scared and wouldn't take his medicine, so I had to allay his fears and persuade him to take the medication.

It was a brief part but for black actors and actresses then, and for the audience, it was very significant because there weren't many black people on television – period.

If you ever did see black people on the TV, they were most likely criminals in the news or, if it was something more positive, they were almost certainly Americans: people like Sidney Poitier, Lena Horne, Ertha Kitt, Harry Belafonte, Sammy Davis or Bill Cosby. So, my landing even that small part in a popular English soap opera was considered a big breakthrough.

In fact, whatever I appeared in during those days in the 1970s was more or less a first, because there was no such thing as 'diversity' or 'multi-racial' casting. The term 'equal opportunities', that we take for granted now, was still a long, long way off.

Later on, we got used to seeing my fellow Trinidadian, Trevor McDonald, reading the news on *News at Ten*, something he did for a very long time.

So, I was one of the first black actresses to appear in *Coronation Street*. Then I got a part in the TV series *Space 1999*, a futuristic space thriller, where I played a doctor, so I was promoted!

But, of course, there was so much time between roles, which were few and far between at the best of time, so it was difficult to think about acting as a full-time career.

It was while I was teaching and occasionally acting, that the BBC launched its first ever black drama series, *Empire Road*, which was set in Birmingham, in the Midlands, north of England.

That show made television history because it was the first time a national TV show on the BBC had portrayed the everyday life story of a black family, and it had peak-time viewing, which was unheard of. That meant that it didn't go out in the 'witching hour' like the few rare programmes at the time that featured black people, and it was on the national broadcast channel, not a local or regional station.

This new show was on at 'tea time' on BBC2; that is in the early evening when families were home and having their evening meal, what the British call their 'tea'. Up to now, people still come up and ask me about *Empire Road*, but, up to this day, I don't know why they didn't commission a longer run. People kept asking for it after the first and second series, but, instead of extending it, the powers that be pulled it from the schedules without any explanation.

But, I should say that although *Empire Road* was the first BBC drama series about a black family on national television, a few years earlier in the 1970s ITV had also made a series called *The Fosters (1976-1977)*, which starred Norman Beaton, Isabelle Lucas, Carmen Munroe and Lenny Henry. It was more a comedy and was made by London Weekend Television, and wasn't put out nationwide.

The Fosters was modelled on an American series called *Good Times,* about a black American family. American television, and cinema for that matter, were always way ahead of the British, so at least the producers of *The Fosters* had an idea that not only was it possible to do something positive with black people in it, but it would also have what they call 'cross-over appeal' — meaning white people could watch it, enjoy it and relate to it in the same way that black people were used to doing with shows that only had white people in them.

On *The Fosters,* Lenny Henry had recently emerged as the new kid on the block after appearing on and winning the TV talent show, *New Faces*, in 1975. Norman was himself getting more established as one of the leading black entertainers and a better-known face on the TV screens by then.

The show was about a black family living in a block of flats in London and it ran for two series. Norman played the father, Samuel Foster and Isabelle played his wife, and Lenny was Sonny, the eldest son.

One thing about Norman was that in real life he had this quick wit and sarcastic sense of humour, and that always came across in the roles he played. He always got the punchlines, anyway, but he could also carry them off because he was a very good actor and a naturally funny comedian and showman. His experience also shone through in that show because they had a lot of new people who were only getting their first chance to appear in a TV show.

Lenny, for example, was only emerging as a stand-up comedian. He was used to appearing on stage in pubs and clubs, and telling jokes. The TV talent show which he won was his launch pad and, with *The Fosters*, he was now moving in a new direction as a comedy-actor on television. So, at least he was given that chance to build on the foundation which he started with.

That is the kind of opportunity which any actor, young or old, would have grabbed with both hands; getting to learn your craft, working on shows with high-production values which were actually being broadcast.

Who could ask for more than that? Well, maybe the only other thing was to have more of the same going on, one after the other rather than having to wait years or even decades before something else came up which you could get the chance to work on.

In some ways the show was like a breath of fresh air at the time because there was nothing else like it anywhere else on our TV screens.

You have to understand that you did not see black people on television very much at all, much less in a series about a family who happened to be black. Mother and father and children in a family unit living everyday lives, doing everyday things like having fun, laughing and joking with each other, sharing a meal, pulling each other's legs; not just complaining about racism or poverty.

It might be a bit much to talk about 'revolutionary', but in many ways it was just like that, because as far as many people in the country were concerned, that was the only way in which they got to see a little into what black people's lives were supposed to be like — although this was only fiction of course.

The alternative was the stuff that appeared in shows where blacks were only stereotyped: doing menial jobs like cleaning or driving buses, or else being muggers, pimps or prostitutes.

Having said that, though, there were still a lot of criticisms from black people about the show, because some people felt that it showed black people in a negative light or that it did not tackle racism or poverty. Some thought it was too lightweight or too trivial, while others felt it wasn't funny enough or 'black' enough, or whatever.

Looking back, you get to realise that, at the best of times, you can't please all the people, all the time. In spite of that, expectations were always high and opportunities were always — and still remain — limited.

So, that was *The Fosters*. Our show, *Empire Road*, ran from 1978-79, and was the first drama written by a black writer, Michael Abbensetts, and starred black actors. I think it had a black audience in mind, although it went out at a time when most of the country would have been watching television with their families.

The directors and producers were white but one episode was directed by the Trinidadian director Horace Ové, who had made the black feature film *Pressure (1975)*, which I had also appeared in.

Norman Beaton was one of the most well-known and talented black actors around at that time. He had won the Variety Club of Great Britain award and was quite well respected in the industry. He was very versatile and could do serious roles as well as comedy, which he was very good at. Many people remember him for *Desmond's*, which came later, in which he played a barber.

Norman was very easy to work with. He was quite a joker and was always telling tall tales. If you told him something he had a funny way of always trying to best you by telling you something outrageous, but he said it in such a serious way that you tended to believe him. It would only be ages, sometimes years later that you would find out he was only pulling your leg and having a laugh at your expense.

In *Empire Road* Norman played Everton Bennett and I played Hortense, his wife. We had a son, Marlon, who was played by the excellent Wayne Laryea, who had been a child actor and was a very talented performer.

In the show, he fell in love with an Asian girl called Narlini, much to the dismay of both sets of parents because love between blacks and Asians was supposed to be taboo.

Love won through in the end, though, and there was an episode of their wedding, which was the only one directed by Horace. It was also one of the best episodes of the entire series. That is because Horace came from a background in photography, so everything looked beautiful; the lighting was fantastic.

Horace is a very good director and photographer and, in my opinion, his primary thing is always making sure what is on the screen looks good. He doesn't forget the acting but his emphasis is on the picture. With Horace you're going to look pretty, but sometimes I think that one needs a little more than that. So, in a way films are better for him than TV because he can get to show off his photography which he is very good at.

I liked *Empire Road* because people could have been more themselves and the characters were very rounded. The stuff we were portraying was true-to-life because we were all black and had experience of West Indian life in the UK. We were making that experience known to a wider audience, so many English people were seeing an all-black cast in realistic roles in a series, for the first time.

The trouble is that as soon as we started to get going and were really getting into the show, they pulled the plug. We made the cover of the *Radio Times*, the BBC's listings magazine, and won a TV award, but somehow that didn't seem to be enough to keep the show going. It always seems to be the same old story: they raise us up and then they let us fall.

They want to know why black people have not gotten any further in what they're doing and I say that if they ask for a black person with a mole on their lip, you better turn up with a mole on your lip because they don't think they can use make-up and put a mole on your lip.

Rather, you have to walk into that audition looking like what they ask for because they don't give you any credit for your acting. It's like they can't imagine anything beyond what is obviously in front of them. Yet a young white actor would turn up and they'll know how to age them up.

For years we were in this country and never got parts unless the role deliberately called for a black character. Unfortunately, most of those parts tended to be cleaners, thieves, muggers, prostitutes or other negative roles.

When parts did start opening up, they called for somebody to sweep the floor or smoke a reefer or pinch somebody's bag, and if you didn't do that as a black actor or actress you didn't get any work.

The director who stepped out beyond that was taking a chance and a few of them did, thank goodness, but the situation hasn't changed that much nowadays. It has a little bit, but not much, because we're still being typecast, but instead of being a garbage man, a black actor is probably driving the truck now, and instead of being the nurse, a black actress is probably the doctor, so that's progress.

I'm not saying there haven't been any changes, there have and you see people getting awards and you think what the hell have they done? I'm a little bit jealous when I see that.

You have to look at the situation of black actors and white actors in Britain. They both start out together. They both move up to a certain point together and then the black actor stops here and the white one goes on up the ladder. Then, they bring in another black actor and start all over again from the beginning with him or her, get to a certain point and then stop them, discard them and bring in someone new to continue the same cycle, so you never make it beyond a certain point. However, the white actor gets a chance to excel.

As I said before, back in the early days there were very few parts for black people on television. As the years went by, despite having the feeling that things were beginning to happen in the industry and opportunities were going to open up for us, we still had to wait years before there was another call to go and audition for something, which might have been very small — working as an extra, for instance; being, not exactly part of a crowd, but maybe having only one or two lines to say.

Coming after you had been in a weekly series with your name at the top of the credits, that could be quite hard to take.

We never had a chance to become famous and we're still not famous. I don't think we will ever become famous, although I always did get fan letters and it's a funny thing because there's a guy in America who always writes and asks for an autograph after everything I've done since I started out.

The first request for autographs came when I was doing *Live and Let Die*, in which I was a dancer, and this fan sent a photograph from the film asking me to autograph it and to see if I could get the autographs of the others if I was in touch with them, but I never got around to doing it. Since then he's followed everything I've done.

Someone asked me why does this fellow keep writing and you don't get back in touch? He even sends a stamped addressed envelope for me to return the stuff in – but I haven't responded. It's flattering to know I have a devoted fan but things like that don't go to my head.

Yes, it was very disappointing when they decided to pull *Empire Road*. It wasn't a roaring success as far as the viewing figures were concerned, but it seemed to be doing very well, considering that BBC2 was in some ways a bit of a TV 'grave yard'.

Norman Beaton stayed with us for a while after the series ended. He was one of a number of actors who lived in our house. Rudolph Walker also stayed with us for a when we were doing the play *Meetings*.

All the performers who stayed in our house always occupied the room at the top.

Chapter Fifteen

Best of Both Worlds

Different actors have their own techniques for learning their lines. I do everything by memory and like to think I have a photographic memory.

If you tell me something, I tend to forget what you tell me but if you write something down for me then I won't forget it. I have to see things written down and not just hear it, otherwise I am hopeless.

How this works with the acting is that if I'm reading a script, I can sit and learn it but if I don't hear the other characters say their parts, then I can't do my part. I learn the script by rote and can picture it in my head. And, if I don't rehearse with the person I'm working with, I fall apart because I have to hear their tone and their pitch and timing. The tone of their voice tells me where I am and what I have to say and do next.

So, sometimes, I don't learn the script, I just have to read it and go to the rehearsal to work with the other characters and as soon as they say what they have to say I know where I am and where I come in. However, if I am just doing a line run with somebody else, not the person I'm acting with, then I'm in real trouble because everybody's tones are different and the tone of the person I'm acting with connects with my brain – it's very odd.

Another thing is I don't like writers directing me. I find that you have to play the part they wrote as they wrote it and depict a part exactly as they envisioned it, which can be one-dimensional. Sometimes it's ideal but sometimes it's not the best that you can get out of the play because when you have a director you have two interpretations, which can be great for bringing out the best out of the writing and the performers. When a writer directs his own work he's too close to it, as far as I'm concerned.

After *Empire Road*, I enjoyed doing *South of the Border* in the late-1980s, which was another BBC series. The show was about a couple of girl detectives, starring Buki Armstrong and Rosie Rowell. It was a bit like a south London version of *Cagney and Lacey*, the popular American show about a pair of women police detectives.

I have always been lucky to have good directors and producers. I can't complain. Again, from time to time I took time off from teaching in the school where I worked and when we wrapped the series or show I was working on, I went back to teaching.

It was a good thing I had the teaching to fall back on and the school where I taught, Southwold Primary School in Hackney, east London, was brilliant and could not have been more supportive. The head mistress made an arrangement with me whereby I could go and do the acting whenever something came up and she would provide cover for my classes.

She told me, "We'll run it like a bank: whenever you have to go off to do your acting I will get in a supply teacher and you won't get paid for those periods. No-one loses; your classes are covered and you get to do your acting and come back to your class when those contracts come to an end."

So, I 'owed' her days when I wasn't around and she 'owed' me days when I was. I made up for the time I took off when I was away acting and stayed there for 20 years.

That arrangement allowed me to have the best of both worlds. I was teaching and had a regular income, so there was none of that humiliating 'signing on the dole': claiming unemployment benefit, during the times that there was no acting work, when actors say they are 'resting'. I taught school and was able to take up parts whenever an acting job came up.

And, it was funny, because parents and children would come in to the school just to look at me because they didn't believe that this teacher was also an actress who sometimes appeared on television.

In time, they got used to it and it wasn't a big deal any more. But, I was one of those teachers who kept them on their toes. I didn't stand for bad behaviour or nonsense. And I was not averse to clipping the naughty ones around the ear. Of course, neither teachers nor parents can do that sort of thing anymore – they'd end up getting arrested.

I never felt strange about having to teach in-between acting parts, and no-one made me feel uncomfortable about the fact that I was on TV one minute and back in the classroom teaching, the next. It was just the way it was. After all, I had to make a living. Leaving the acting and going into a classroom didn't make any difference to me. If show business people felt any way about me doing that, then that was their problem.

The other reason that I think the school liked that arrangement was because 80 percent of the children in that school were black or from another 'ethnic minority' but there were no black teachers, so the head was making a point in trying to retain me to help motivate the children.

I got on well with the children. I disciplined them when it was time for discipline (of course you dare not do that nowadays) and celebrated them when it was time for praise.

The other teachers used to wonder how I managed to get them to behave and produce good work. I didn't pander to the children, which is what most of the others were doing but that didn't get their respect. I still meet people I used to teach and they greet me and remind me of how I used to be their teacher. It is always intriguing to see how they turned out.

I think the other thing that worked for me during that time was the fact that when I was acting I would never worry about whether I would get another acting job or not. I never had that anxiety because Trevor always worked and I had a 'back up' job in teaching.

I used to say, "Trevor works for the bread and butter and I do acting for the jam."

Some people go into auditions fraught and desperate to get the job because they are out of work. That never happened to me because I was never depending on acting for my livelihood. I didn't consider it a lesser role or a distraction to be teaching in a classroom if I didn't get a part I had auditioned for.

South of the Border came along at a good time for me and I enjoyed doing the show, which wasn't re-commissioned after the first run.

When it ended, I was getting ready to go to South Africa with some good friends, Jean and Nat, who were going there for a holiday. This was while Apartheid was going on and Nelson Mandela was still imprisoned. We'd been on other holidays together to places like Greece and Spain. So we booked our tickets but just before we were due to go, I got a call to go up for the TV series, *Rides*.

I didn't have to audition; they just called me and asked me if I wanted to do it. I had to cancel my trip to South Africa, which I was pleased about because in my head there were three places I had never wanted to visit: South Africa, Australia and Israel. If you can see a link between those places you will see where I'm coming from with this.

I didn't want to go to any country where they didn't like me as a black person but would tolerate me and, to me, South Africa, Australia and Israel were like that.

Although I had booked to go, I hated the idea of visiting South Africa because of apartheid. We had adopted a family through the African National Congress (ANC) and used to support them by sending money once a month.

So, I was relieved to have been offered a part in *Rides*, a show about a group of women taxi drivers. I was one of the drivers and my 'run' was by the Strand in central London.

In the storyline there was a set up where each of the taxi drivers had a storyline and I always felt good about that part because it was a positive image of a black woman who was independent and in control, not a victim or a criminal.

After that I also did two episodes of the detective series *Lovejoy*. One episode was with Rudolph Walker, who played my husband, and Diane Parish, who played our daughter.

I've worked with Diane about three or four times, on TV and on stage. I also worked quite a lot with the actress Mona Hammond (whose name was Mavis Chin). I have known her since she was at drama school, attending RADA.

At one stage, many, many years ago, she used to dance with Allistair Bain's dance group. As a matter of fact, I met Mona through Allistair and in our dancing days she even stayed with us when I lived in Finchley. And, much later, she stayed with us for about a week after we'd done a play in Scotland called *As Time Goes By,* an award-winning play by Mustapha Matura, which also starred Stefan Kalipha.

I did one episode of *Black Silk,* which starred Rudolph Walker as a black barrister. The character was based on a real lawyer called Rudy Narayan, who was a very dynamic and controversial personality and a first-class lawyer. A young actor called Sylvester Williams played one of my sons.

I have done so much work with Rudolph, both on stage and on TV. We worked together on *Empire Road, Casualty,* something called *Brighton Boy,* and the plays *Meetings, A Dying Business,* and *Black Man's Burden.*

Rudolph and my brother, Mervyn, knew each other from school but, up until about three years ago, Rudolph did not know that Mervyn was my brother.

I also knew Lorna, Rudolph's first wife very well. Rudolph used to hang around with a group of us performers who were who were always coming together at socials held by a woman called Alma Tanuke, who was a very good friend and a socialite who knew just about everyone who was involved in the arts.

It was at Alma's that I met the South African singer Miriam Makeba. Alma was a hairdresser and everybody that came from Trinidad, from the Prime Minister down, used to go to Alma's and that's where a lot of the actors, dancers and musicians also ended up.

In the sixties they brought a show called *King Kong* from South Africa, and they performed in the West End. It was the first South African group to come here and perform and Miriam Makeba and Pearl Connor's husband, Joseph Mogotsi (whom she married after she split with Edric Connor), came with the show and he and some others didn't go back home to S.A.

The actress Nimmy March's father was one of those who came with that show. It was only years later that she found out who her father was, because she was adopted as a baby by aristocrats the Earl of March and his wife.

Years later, Nimmy traced her family tree and went to South Africa to find her father. Imagine that, I knew him all the time, although I didn't know he had a daughter who was adopted.

Nimmy was the celebrated new talent in the 1980s. She was in so many things on television and then you ended up wondering where she was and what she was doing because you didn't see her in anything any more.

As I said before, that is what happens to black people in the UK. White performers continue to go up and up, but we never, ever, ever, get to the top. They cut you off three quarters of the way up so we never get the chance to make it all the way to the top.

I can't say that nobody has managed to make it, but compared to the white ones who started at the same time there are very, very few that actually go all the way. I suppose someone like Lenny Henry went all the way up the ladder, but on the other hand he went up the ladder as a comedian; that can happen with him doing his own shows, he didn't have to depend on their plays to get him noticed.

He is the so-called top black comedian, but I don't know if he's funny because he's not my thing, so I can't judge him. But, if you think of the black actors, how many of them have gone to the top and at the end of the year when they are sending up people for the BAFTAs and so on actually get to go there?

If someone is a singer they might get there, but if they are an actor, then no way. The problem starts because they are not being put up for the parts that count. Sometimes you also have to depend on the public to vote for you and when that's the case the black actors won't get there.

Marianne Jean-Baptiste, who did really well in the film *Secrets and Lies (1996)*, is an example of someone who has done very well for herself in the industry, especially now she has gone to the United States.

The very first thing she appeared in was something called *Island Life*, which we did together at the Lyric Theatre in Hammersmith, west London.

She was still at RADA at the time, and later I went to see the performance that she did for her graduation. She is a fantastic singer and someone with many strings to her bow.

I can carry a tune and I have sung in plays, but I wouldn't stand up tomorrow and call myself a singer. I sang in *Amen Corner* and there was one play that I did called *Don't Chat me Business* where I had to sing a hymn acapella and they were surprised that every night I sang that song in the right key without any music. Angela winter was in that play as well.

After *Island Life* I did *Running Dream* at Stratford East and Marianne was in that as well and I still have a picture of her sitting on my lap. Lenny Henry also did a play called *The Man* and both Marianne and I were in that.

I also worked a lot with Ellen Thomas, both on stage and TV and I worked with the broadcaster and performer Alex Pascall when he first came to this country. Back then, he was a drummer.

We both used to work together a lot with Allistair Bain, who did a lot of dancing before, like me, he got into the acting and even appeared in an episode or two of *Empire Road.*

As an actress I am forever playing people's mums. In my early days I used to play my age range but in my later years I found myself playing mothers and grandmothers.

More than twenty years after I played a mum in my first regular TV series, *Empire Road* on the BBC, I would soon find myself picking up my apron and rubber gloves once again to play a matriarch in one of British television's most popular shows.

Chapter Sixteen

Eastenders

Just before I did *Eastenders*, the most popular soap opera on British television, I went home to Trinidad, as I normally did every year. That was in 1999.

When I returned to England, I did the James Baldwin play, *Amen Corner*, which started at the Tricycle theatre in London and was transferred to the Nottingham Playhouse, in the north of England.

I have done *Amen Corner* twice: the first time with Carmen Munroe and Clarke Peters, who is now a big international film and TV star. He was in it originally, and so was Sylvester Williams.

When we did the first production we actually had the writer, James Baldwin, there with us. He was a lovely man; really, really nice.

There was a fire at the Tricycle and when they refurbished the place they named one of the rooms after James Baldwin – The James Baldwin Room. That was before he died.

So, I was doing *Amen Corner* and just as I finished doing the play we had the auditions for *Eastenders*. I got a call and the agent sent me along. I didn't know the show because I didn't use to watch it at the time, although my cousin Lorna (whom I call my sister) watched it religiously and used to give me a full run down of the storylines.

Eastenders is big, no doubt about it. Just mention the theme tune and everyone knows the show. My favourite programme at that time was *Coronation Street*, which was like a rival to *Eastenders*.

I went along to the audition with a script but I had no idea what to expect. Yvonne Brewster, the actress and theatre director, was also there for the audition, and so were a number of other people whom I recognised. So, the competition was quite fierce.

My attitude, however, was: well, one of us has to get it and if it's me, that's good, but if not, then so be it. I couldn't get myself too worked up. What would have been the point?

Certainly, it's a plum show to be on because you're watched by millions of people three or four times a week and it also gets seen all over the world, but I tried to keep my cool.

A number of black actors and actresses have done *Eastenders* in the past, including Oscar James, Mona Hammond and, I think, Joan Hooley, who was one of the first black actresses in a TV series on television in Britain back in the 1960s.

Once you do that show, your premium goes up because you become a bit of a household name, even if people only know your character's name.

Back in the early 1990s, they had a black family — the Taverniers — in the show. Come to think of it, that was probably the first major representation of a black family unit by the BBC after *Empire Road*.

The Taverniers featured Tommy Eytle (who was a musician before getting into acting), Leroy Golding, Jacqui Gordon-Lawrence, Steve Woodcock, and Michelle Gayle, who went on to have a successful singing career.

Like all the other families in the show, they had their ups and downs, and, as usual, it was not possible to please all the people all the time. Some liked them, some didn't; some thought they didn't get a big enough role or were realistic enough. Still, as far as some were concerned, at least they had black people in the show.

Anyway, long after that family had moved out or whatever, it seems they were introducing another black family into the series.

I went along and did the audition and they said 'yes'. It was really exciting then, and I grabbed the opportunity with both hands.

My character was a woman called Audrey Trueman, who was very independent and enterprising. She ran a bed and breakfast motel in Albert Square, where the show is set.

Soon after that first audition, I went along for another interview where they were choosing the characters that would be in my family. Nicholas Bailey got the part as my steady doctor son and they had us in workshops to get us used to some storylines before launching us into the show.

Gary Beadle was chosen some time later to play my other 'son', who was a rebellious, prodigal called Paul. He didn't come in at the beginning. I'm not quite sure whether Gary did the workshops but we were already filming when he came in.

I had worked with Gary before on a BBC children's show called *Murphy's Mob*, and then we worked on something else which was about a nightclub, although I can't remember what it was called.

He is a very talented actor who had started out in children's theatre. He was already quite experienced and is very good at his craft, something that shone through on *Eastenders*.

That was the second time that I had done a series where I was chosen first and then they chose my 'family'. They had done that with *South of the Border* back in the 1980s.

My first contract was for six months with an option to do a further six. In the storyline, my family was going to be doing a lot of interacting with another new family called the Slaters, and one of the girls would become very friendly with one of my sons.

At home, my cousin Lorna would fill me in on the different storylines so that I knew the background of what was happening in the show. Working on *Eastenders* was a lot different to other things I had done before. With all the shows I had done before we used to have rehearsals, so you went to the rehearsals and you did your thing and you were fairly relaxed about it all.

I must also say in those other series we did an episode a week but in *Eastenders* we did three episodes at a go and there was no such thing as rehearsals, which were replaced by run-throughs.

The episodes were filmed a long time in advance and it wasn't difficult but the fact that we had no rehearsals was a bit daunting for me. They just give you your script, and then call you in on the morning of the day they're setting up and you read your script and that was it. Then you go back to your dressing room.

When you go back to the set, you better go there knowing your script because that's it: you have a run-through and then it's a take. You get on the set and they show you your position and everybody says their lines and then you're in position. The lighting is in place but that rehearsal is not for you, it's a technical rehearsal. The only rehearsal that you have is when you got together with the others in your scene and said your lines. So that was different because I had always been used to doing other series and plays where we had at least two weeks' rehearsal time.

I had done episodes in drama series like *The Bill*, *Casualty* and things like that where they sent you the script and then forget about you until the day of the shoot when you would turn up prepared.

With this show, you had to be on your toes and make up your mind that you weren't going to be the one to fluff your lines, which would make you very uncomfortable.

My colleagues on *Eastenders* were generous. There were few people there who were selfish. Some, like the actress June Brown, who played the odd-ball but iconic character Dot Cotton, was extremely good. June has been on the show practically from the beginning and she was the best person on that set as far as I was concerned. She is such a lovely person.

The nicest person I've ever worked with on any production during my career was Helen Mirren. We were doing *Prime Suspect Two*, the TV drama that really launched her into Hollywood status. You know, there are some people who are just wonderful and there are some who are not unfriendly, but they don't go out of their way to help or acknowledge you.

Helen Mirren was nice and very helpful. Although she was a big star, she didn't have any airs and graces, and she was thoroughly supportive to me.

I had a very emotional scene to do and we didn't have any rehearsals.

She said to me, "You're not going to get time to work up an emotion, so you'll have to come on the set ready for the take."

And she explained it to me, which the director should have done but probably didn't have time to do.

I don't even think that she knew how much that meant to me. Of course, she was making sure that I didn't spoil her performance as well, but it was more than that, she was actually doing something very generous.

I've come to the conclusion that the bigger the stars are the more friendly they are in a way because I had that same thing when I did a production with Vanessa Redgrave's sister, Lynn, years ago at the BBC.

On stage you get all the directions, you put in the emotion and so on. But, on television, it doesn't happen any more and many directors don't seem to have the time or make the effort to motivate and inspire the actors unless they are the star.

When I did *Empire Road* years ago, we had days and even weeks of rehearsals. And for *South of the Border* I used to go down to the BBC studio in Acton, west London, and rehearse every morning for weeks before we actually started filming. Those were the days. Little did we know that drama would get cut down to brass tacks and rehearsals would become a luxury that no production can afford any longer.

I didn't mind the part I played in *Eastenders*, it was OK, but there was no excitement to the character. Audrey was simply a woman of a certain age and the mother of grown-up children, and she was trying to run a business in a small community where people's loyalties would shift at the drop of a hat.

One day, the producers asked me and Nicholas to go to a workshop where they were doing readings with about six or seven people, including Rudolph Walker and they came back and told me that he had got the part.

They said, "Oh, you and Rudolph will work well together."

So I said, "Well, we have worked together quite a lot of times."

Rudolph was supposed to have been my husband in the show, but he and I were estranged. We hadn't divorced but I'd left him and Gary, who played Paul, my eldest son, was not Rudolph's child. Rudolph's character was still in Trinidad not doing so well while I was there in Albert Square making good for myself by running a bed and breakfast business.

However, the two of us never did work together on that show because he only came along after I'd been killed off. I don't think my death was something they had planned originally. I think that came about because they wanted to get me off the show. My reason for saying so is that I got a script and it was awful.

I phoned up Nick and said, "Have you read your script?"

And he said, "Yea."

So, I said, "I'm not doing that."

And he said, "Oh, I don't know what we can do about it."

I felt strongly about the script because I felt it was degrading.

The storyline was that I'd arrived from Trinidad and there were no jobs around so I took a job cleaning toilets in Waterloo station and I rose from doing that to owning my bed and breakfast motel.

All that came out because they were trying to tell another character, Barry Evans, who was out of a job at the time, that he could take anything going because, look at how Audrey had started from being a toilet cleaner to owning her own business! It was supposed to be motivating to him, but I found it degrading to me.

So, I turned up at the studio and spoke to a mixed-race girl who was one of the producers working that particular day.

I told her, "I'm not saying those lines."

And she said, "Do you object?"

And I said, "Yes."

I spoke to the casting director and the producer and told them that I did not want to do to say the lines as they were written.

I told them straight, "I'm not doing that."

I could start from anything else but not a toilet cleaner. You are telling the people that I came all the way from Trinidad and I was educated but took a job cleaning toilets. I agreed that that you could be educated and take a job below your ambition but I didn't want my character cleaning any toilets! Give me another job, any job, but not one cleaning toilets!

I was getting a whole lot of fan mail by then and I felt like it was a case of the black woman comes on the television and all she can talk about is being a toilet cleaner? Please!

I'm saying to myself, now what sort of image am I giving these little black children who are watching this show? Am I telling them to go and clean toilets? Come on, you don't get on the television and tell people you were a toilet cleaner, even if it is only a drama. It sounds derogatory and although it might not be a big thing to some people, it was a big thing to me.

So, I refused to do that and they changed the script. They didn't show any annoyance, they said that they understood. If they objected, they didn't show it. That was after my second contract but when my third came up for review they called me down to the office one day and told me that they had a script that they thought was a really good script and they can't really refuse it. They began to tell me about this 'lovely script'. It was the script in which I got killed, so I was being written out of the show.

So I said, "Oh, how am I getting killed?"

Well, they had some scaffolding at the Queen Vic, the pub in the heart of the show where all the action happens, and I'm standing outside looking at something or the other and turn back suddenly and bump my head on the scaffolding and then I collapse. Then I got home and died because I got an aneurysm. That sounds exciting, doesn't it? A really 'lovely script'.

I could be wrong, but I put it down to the fact that I had challenged the story about me being a toilet cleaner. They had me down to work with Rudolph and they still wanted the B&B in the show so they killed me off and brought Rudolph in to take over.

In the storyline that caused a problem because in my will I had left the B&B to Paul, who was a scamp. Anyway, Rudolph's character came in, pussyfooted with Paul and eventually got the business from him.

I think they killed me off because they couldn't be sure about what I might object to doing in the future. Perhaps they thought I was 'difficult'. I have no regrets because I have left with my image intact. It is a big thing because millions of people see the show.

Only recently, I went to a football match and a white couple with their two small children came up to me and said, "Ah, we miss you in *Eastenders*."

I went to the USA for Obama's inauguration and there were people there who spotted me in the crowd and came up to congratulate me for my role in *Eastenders*, so it has gone out worldwide.

Anyway, I'm not sorry because I hear a lot of people saying things about other people how they shouldn't have done something in a show. You have to make the best of what you get to do with the parts you are given and don't degrade yourself.

The long and the short of it is that I didn't get to work with Rudolph on *Eastenders*, but I've worked with him before on lots of things, so that wasn't a problem. Anyway, they brought Angela Wynter in to be his wife, and Angela and I have worked on a number of things before as well.

Diane Parish is also in the show now and I have played her mother in a number of productions.

Interestingly, Rudolph and I worked with Angela on the very first thing that she did, which was a play called *Meetings,* at the Hampstead Theatre. Rudolph played my husband and she played a little girl from the country who comes to be the servant. We worked on other things as well, including a production called *Zombie*, where we did a lot of travelling to different theatres.

Angela did *Eastenders* for about eight years and then Rudolph's character divorced her. They cut out people in such a strange way. And I am so angry with them for not putting up Gary Beadle for a soap award for his role in *Eastenders*.

That young man is such a talented actor and he was absolutely brilliant in the episode where I died. He was just fantastic. People from the studio came and applauded him when he'd finished doing his take. It was so intense that while we were shooting the whole studio was quiet and people came from other sets to watch, and he never even got a mention for that sterling work.

I'm so pissed off about that because he deserved a nomination at least. That show is so bad it's unbelievable, but that's my story. Some people might say it's just sour grapes.

At the end of the day, it's only a job; you've got to remember that. To some people, being on television can seem like a pleasant and extraordinary thing to do, but the hardest part is sitting around a lot of the time and just waiting. You spend hours, sometimes days filming something that is on screen for only a few seconds, and sometimes your scene ends up on the cutting room floor.

It is interesting that I started on the BBC with *Empire Road* and ended with *Eastenders*.

When my agent, Jan Evans, retired I felt sure that was the end for me because I doubt that I will get another agent at this stage in my life.

My first agent, Chris O'Neil, moved to Wales and when he relocated he just kept eight of us on his books, including myself and Nina Baden-Semper. And then a few years later he had a sheep farm and decided he was going to retire altogether. When he did, I didn't get alarmed or worried because producers were calling me and casting agents were calling me directly to offer roles.

I didn't actually go looking for an agent, but eventually I ended up on the books of Jan Evans and we had a good run. Actors don't really retire in this business, although the agents do, and the reason I think she packed it in was because work is so hard to get because most of the work that's going now are reality TV shows.

Once in a while they get you something but it got so bad that now they're not even using trained actors for a lot of things, they're picking up anybody that looks 'right' because it's cheaper for them. So it's difficult and expensive for agents to run an office with staff.

I retired from the teaching some time ago back in 1996, and I keep saying that I'm only doing cameos: small acting parts, no large roles. Yes, it's limiting but in my view that's better than going out there and making a fool of myself.

The first thing people will say is, "Oh, God, why doesn't she give it up, she can't remember her lines!"

With *The Emperor Jones*, the Eugene O'Neill play I did at the Gate Theatre, the agent sent me up for it and I got the part. That was a good production to work on, otherwise I wouldn't have done it. The play later transferred to the National Theatre.

Many black people hate that play. When I read the script at first I didn't like it but – you see there are some things that I don't like and I don't do, and there are some things that I don't like, but I do.

What I object to are productions that make me look like a fool. But plays like *The Emperor Jones* are historical. That was how people behaved in the past but we have moved on from those days. That's how it happened then and there's nothing that you could do about it so, therefore, in that respect, I don't object. But, if they were giving me a part today to be a bloody coon, then I'm not doing it.

Years ago, there was a part that I turned down. I'm not going to tell you who it was but I'm just going to explain what happened. I went to the BBC to audition for something.

I met a friend after the interview and told her, "I'm going to get that part but I don't want it."

I knew when I was being auditioned that I was going to get the part, so I'd said to them, "I'm not too sure that I'm going to be around because I'm going on holiday."

Sure enough, by the time I got home, my agent rang and said, "Corinne, you've got the part, but I didn't know you were going on holiday."

I said, "Yes, I am."

So he said, "Where are you going?"

I said, "Switzerland."

So he said, "Oh, OK, I'll tell them."

He rang them and then rang me back. They told him that they would offer me X amount of money – way more than the going rate – if I would cancel my trip so that I could do the part.

Neil rang me at the school and said, "Corinne, the BBC said that they'll pay your passage to come back from Switzerland. They really want you for this part."

At that time I had not booked to go anywhere but I said, "No, I can't do it because I've made arrangements."

Now, my husband Trevor had a cousin, Jean, who worked at the Trinidad Embassy in Switzerland, and I rang her and said, "Jean, I'm coming for a visit."

She was delighted and said, "Yes, yes, come."

So, by the time Neil rang back I told him I had to leave England for a certain amount of days and I left the country.

The part the BBC wanted me for was to play somebody's mother and I didn't like the character and definitely did not want to play their mother. I thought no, I'm not doing that. Even now, although so much time has passed, I still won't say what the play was.

I left the country because I didn't want to do the role but I didn't want to fall out with the BBC; so they'd be thinking, "Oh, she thinks she's so big she can refuse this part."

Not only that, but the BBC worked on a scale and every time you did something you went up on the scale so I went up because I'd done so many things with them, thank you very much, and I didn't want them to cut me off.

The teachers at the school were saying to me, "But Corinne, you should have done it," and so on, but when they saw the play when it was televised they all said they were glad I didn't do it.

Another thing: I did *A Touch of Frost*, a popular television show starring David Jason. When I went for that interview that part called for me to play a woman who was a prostitute, and quite a few people went for the audition dressed in character but I didn't; I just went as I was. I got the part.

And when I saw the script, you would have realised that it wasn't an obvious prostitute, a street walker. The storyline was that a person got killed and they accused my grandson of the crime but it wasn't him. He was innocent and they came to my house to search it because they suspected that, on top of being a killer, he had stolen a lot of things. But when they came in and looked around they found a lot of expensive goods which I had got because I worked as a hooker and got paid with gifts instead of cash.

So, that was what I did in *A Touch of Frost*, and that one earned me the most royalties, funnily enough, because every time they brought out a new series, they always showed that first episode.

David Jason, the star of the show, was good to work with but you didn't really see him much. He was so busy, you know, one of those guys that is doing this and running here and doing that. You didn't really socialise with him on the set, although you got to hang out with the rest of the cast.

On top of the parts that I accepted, there were a lot of parts that I objected to. Usually it's my instinct that tells me that a part doesn't feel right, so then I don't do it.

Another thing that I don't like is that if I go to see a play and I like it, I stay back and say hello to the people and tell them what I liked and didn't. But, if I see a play that's horrible from beginning to end, I don't wait around.

After that play finishes, I'm the first one out the door because I'm not going to stand up there and pretend: "Oh, that was fantastic!", when it wasn't. Before I have to say that, I just leave. I won't be a hypocrite.

Chapter Seventeen

The Other Woman

Trevor started teaching at Brook House Boys' School in Hackney, east London, in 1972. He was there for a number of years and, eventually, he was promoted to head of department for Social Studies.

Of course, all the time he was teaching he was still very actively involved in his political activities and community development issues, and he had excellent contributions to make in these areas.

And, for him, teaching was not just a job, it was a vocation; something he was very much committed to.

He really gave it his all and he felt he had made the right decision to commit to teaching rather than architecture, which had been his first choice. In the early 1980s, Trevor became a Fellow of the Institute of Education at the University of London.

It was around the late seventies and early eighties that scores of black boys, in particular, were being excluded from schools and sent to so-called 'sin bins' or units for what they termed 'educationally sub-normal' juveniles.

All this was linked to delinquency and black children were being labelled with such negative stereotypes and accused of underachieving very badly in the schools. It really was a crying shame.

As a result of some political pressures to look into this 'underachievement', the government set up an enquiry and Trevor was asked to be part of the team leading it called *The Swann Committee*.

It was headed by Lord Swann, a former BBC chairman and education specialist. Trevor considered it a great honour to be part of that commission and made a valuable contribution to it.

The Swann Report, which was published in 1985 as '*Education for All*', was the first major report on the issue of education and black, or 'ethnic minority children' (as they termed them), in Britain.

It was really significant, especially because, for the first time ever, it was officially recommended that the educational curriculum should be multi-cultural and reflect the ethnic background of the children in the schools. This was a whole new development and the impact was electrifying.

Trevor was given a fellowship and later he was offered the MBE (Member of the British Empire), which he turned down.

There were two reasons why he refused it. He said that one reason was because Margaret Thatcher, the Prime Minister, pooh-poohed the report when it came out and the other reason was that they were saying, 'Member of the British Empire' when Britain didn't have an empire any more. So, he refused the award.

As far as Trevor was concerned it was going to be an embarrassment for him to have the accolade because of his political affiliations. There was some coverage about that in the West Indian press but not in the mainstream press because I don't think they knew anything about it.

At the time I was teaching at a school in Hackney and my colleagues were excited that Trevor had been offered the MBE and said he should have taken it. I told them it was up to him.

Of course, this all came about at a very difficult time in the society, because there were riots in places like Brixton and Tottenham, in London, and Toxteth, Liverpool, in the north of England.

Margaret Thatcher's government was giving people a hard time politically and economically and I think some people just decided they'd had enough of living inside a society that was like a pressure cooker and the lid just blew off.

Black people were in the newspapers for all the wrong reasons: throwing petrol bombs, looting shops, attacking police and running riot.

It was not exactly the image we had for ourselves and many of us found it hard to understand or relate to that type of militant reaction against the authorities, although Trevor was less surprised and critical about the whole thing than I was.

After *The Swann Report,* he got a job as a Community Liaison Officer at the Inner London Education Authority (ILEA), the education authority for London that was part of the Greater London Council (GLC). After some years, he worked his way up to become ILEA's Head of Equal Opportunities.

It was around this time that he met Jean, a fellow educationalist who was helping him to write his book, *Shattering Illusions: West Indians in British Politics*, which was being published by Lawrence & Wishart.

The book deal was a high point for Trevor. It gave him the opportunity to combine his love and knowledge of education and politics and to present his views to the world exactly the way he wanted them presented.

As soon as he started doing the book he used to be out most nights and, during the day, he was working with ILEA, so things were pretty busy for him, and I think he liked it like that. In many ways he was in his element.

It was while he was Head of Equal Opportunities that they sent him to the USA on a fact-finding mission to visit different schools in New York. He was given a plaque by the city's Mayor, which he felt very pleased about.

He also went to California on another one of those visits and was making quite a name for himself as an authority on the education of black children in the UK.

This was around the mid-1980s when so much was happening socially and politically: there were serious challenges for the country under the Conservative government of Prime Minister Margaret Thatcher with policies like the Poll Tax and selling off council houses.

But, having said that, a lot of creative doors were also opening up with things like the start of Channel Four Television which promised new opportunities for black people and other minorities.

Well, aside from that, my husband had a book deal and his own friendly editor, Jean, on call to help him put his mountains of ideas and analysis down on paper.

He and Jean were always working on the book together. They had deadlines to meet, stuff to go over, amendments to make, a manuscript to finish. So, it was no wonder they were always in each other's pockets around that time.

On the surface it seemed perfectly reasonable, perfectly legitimate; they were busy on a project. While he was working on the book Trevor was very upbeat, pleasant, happy and firing on all cylinders.

Of course, we were very supportive and gave him all the time and space he needed to do his work. Sometimes, Jean would come to our house or he would go to her's, and when anybody asked where he was we would say, "Oh, he's with his book buddy" or his 'book mark', as we referred to her.

That became our in-joke. I meant it quite innocently but I had no idea that the joke was on me. I didn't think anything about the two of them being together, stupid as I was.

Around that time Trevor always went out and always stayed out late and always came back in at whatever time he pleased, but it was not a problem. He was always a night person in any case, so I had no reason to suspect him of anything untoward whenever he came in during the early hours of the morning, having been out all evening.

Stupid me. But not only was Jean having an affair with my husband, but some time later she became pregnant with his child.

They both worked at ILEA and I later learned that he used to take her out a lot, but not to any of the places where I went or around any of the people that I knew, although some of his friends knew her and knew about the affair.

I suppose he passed her off as his work colleague or whatever, or maybe there was a 'nudge-nudge', 'wink-wink' kind of thing going on with some of his set.

In any event, I was foolishly ignorant that my man had another woman and was parading her around behind my back.

Anyway, when the book was finished we thought, 'Great!' (and even now it is still being sold and money comes in from time to time for royalties).

The book came out around the time that I was doing a play called *Remembrance (1980)* by Derek Walcott, which was very prescient in many ways.

The play happened to be running over a carnival bank holiday weekend in London, which takes place at the end of August.

Apparently, Trevor came to one of the performances but didn't stay; he slipped away afterwards, so I didn't even know that he'd been in the audience.

Interestingly, the play was about relationships and secrets, but, unknown to me, that same thing was going on in my own family although I was the last one to know.

We had one of my cousins, Myrna, visiting on holiday. Before she left to go back to Trinidad she told my other cousin, Lorna, who was living with us at the time , about Trevor's affair.

Lorna was my first cousin. We had grown up together in the same house as children when my mother died, and we were raised as sisters.

We also looked alike and people used to mistake Lorna for me and me for her. Some even thought we were twins. We got a kick out of that. She was four years younger than me and had been four-years-old, the same age as my brother, Leo, when our mum died.

Lorna's mother died when she was eight and I was twelve, and our grandmother brought us up after that. She's the one who brought my daughter, Dian-Marie, to me in England some years later.

Dian-Marie was six, nearly seven, when she came here, and, at first she used to look to Lorna as her mother because she knew more about Lorna than me. Remember, when I had left Trinidad she was still a baby, so that was only to be expected.

So, anyway, Lorna knew the secret about my husband's other woman. It also transpired that Claire, Trevor's sister, also knew.

Talk about secrets and lies! I seemed to be the only one who didn't know anything. I tell you the truth: ignorance is not bliss.

That was the August. Then, suddenly, Lorna and Trevor were always having rows in the house. I didn't know why and I don't think he realised why they were always rowing, because I don't think he knew that she knew about his infidelity.

She was arguing with him because she knew about his 'outside white woman' but she never told him so. Instead, she found no end of excuses to pick a fight with him.

They always seemed to be at each other's throats. I found it strange that they no longer got on, but didn't really get involved because I thought it was just a passing thing and that, like all families, they would work out their differences.

Trevor would always refer to her as 'your sister'. He was somewhat resentful of how close we were and it must have infuriated him that we all lived in the same house. I'm sure he thought, rightly, that I was closer to her than I ever was to him.

I think by about the November or early December that year all these people knew about the affair but I was completely ignorant. Everyone seemed to know except me.

It must have been just before Christmas when it all came out: Trevor told me about the affair. At first I was numb with shock and then, I threw up. I had never vomited before in my life. I can put my hand down my throat but I can't make myself vomit, and even when I was pregnant I never experienced morning sickness. But when Trevor told me about Jean and that she was pregnant, I threw up. And that was the first and last time.

Anyway, Christmas came and went. Old year's night — New Year's Eve — came and we went to a party. He and Lorna had the most awful row right there in the party. My stomach was churning like you wouldn't believe. We drove back home and the following morning I packed a suitcase.

Trevor wasn't there, he'd gone out. I put the suitcase in the car and took some presents from under the Christmas tree. After that I went upstairs to speak to Lorna, who didn't know that I knew about the affair.

I didn't let on, I just told her, "I'm going to take Pony's present to their family in Muswell Hill."

Pony was a family friend going back many, many years.

When I got there, his wife, Claire, knew about the affair. Apparently, Trevor had gone there to ask Pony's advice about what he should do, or something stupid like that. So, they had also known about it. And all these people who knew had given him a mouthful, and he was in a state.

Another friend was so angry that she told him, "Don't bring that woman anywhere near me or I won't be responsible for my actions!"

I booked myself into a hotel not far from where we lived, and told myself that I was not going back home until I had got my head together. But, before going to the hotel I went to see some other friends, Jean and Nat. Jean said, "No, don't go to the hotel, stay here tonight and if you still feel like it then go to the hotel in the morning."

Anyway, I stayed the night with them and the following day Jean gave me a lift to the hotel. That means that I didn't go home the Saturday night, Sunday, or the Monday, and, apparently, when I hadn't been home for all that time Trevor made the mistake of asking Lorna if she knew where I was.

That did it! She was so angry that she grabbed an old umbrella she had upstairs and beat him up with it. Our son, Mick, had to go and rescue Trevor because Lorna was so furious there's no telling what damage she could have inflicted.

The cat was now well and truly out of the bag. Dian-Marie was in a state, she was so upset. She kept saying that it was her fault that her step-father had done what he did because she was not his biological child.

The whole house was in confusion but nobody knew where I was. This was now the early part of January and the school where I worked was due to re-open after the Christmas holidays. Unable to track me down, Trevor phoned the school to see if they knew where I was.

They eventually found me and I went back home to have a meeting with the family. Trevor was talking rubbish about, "Jean is into children and she can't have an abortion" and all these stories. He even came out with how he "didn't know she would get pregnant" because I had my menopause and he thought he was having his menopause too. Have you ever heard shit like that? Here was a man, a big stupid man, talking like that.

After that Trevor went back to work and had a nervous breakdown. Isn't it ironic? He was the one doing all the damage to the family but he was the one who had the breakdown and, sudden, he was the centre of attention again because everyone started to feel sorry for him.

We had to send him off to Switzerland for treatment. He had a cousin working at the Trinidad and Tobago High Commission over there, so she put him up.

We had to pick up the pieces and carry on. It's funny, because I used to go to Archway to shop and there was a shop right by the corner where I used to buy my meat. Jean used that same butcher, but after she got pregnant I have never, never, never seen her there again. Twenty-one years have gone by and I have never seen her and yet she is just living up the road from us.

That stupid man went and had an affair right on his own doorstep. You could say right under my nose, since she used to come to our house or he would go to hers, and I never suspected a thing.

It's not really about forgiving her, it's about forgiving Trevor, although it takes two to tango. My friends never forgave him and my cousin Lorna never spoke to him again.

Although the two of them still lived in the same house they never had a conversation after his affair. If it wasn't a row, it was seething silence. She cut him off and merely grunted in his direction if she had to communicate with him at all. You can just imagine the tension.

I didn't think about leaving him but I thought about putting him out. I reasoned that I didn't do anything wrong, so why should I go? In the end, I decided he had to go but he begged me to stay.

He said that Jean wanted him to leave me and go to her and I told him to go to her.

I shouted, "Go on, she'll have you!"

Whether he was procrastinating or not I have no idea but he made no attempts to move out, although, far from trying to stop him I actually encouraged him to leave; to get out of my life and go to his white woman since that was what he obviously wanted.

He was a hypocrite talking black but sleeping white. He said the woman wanted him to leave me for them to be a family, but he didn't want that. He said he wanted to save his marriage.

Trevor was always lacking in confidence and suffered from low self-esteem. I think he had always had an inferiority complex. Perhaps the relationship with this white career woman gave him a sense of achievement, who knows?

Anyway, his mistress had a baby girl and they named her Claudia, perhaps after Claudia Jones, Trevor's cousin.

But, once the dust had settled in our house, none of the family ever spoke about the affair again. Everyone carried on as though it never happened. To think, a blabbering family keeping mum (excuse the pun) about something as soul destroying as that.

In the end, he didn't leave and I got tired of trying to make him go. We may have been sharing a house, but as far as friendship and intimacy went, the marriage was definitely over.

A lot of people couldn't understand why I settled for what I did and a few used to tell me, "Girl, you're putting up with a lot of things that I would not stand for."

Later on, over the years, Trevor wanted us to meet the child and would tell me that he had shown the child my picture. What was he showing her my picture for? She was nothing to do with me, she was to do with him.

She was nothing to do with us, with our family. I used to tell him it was a shame what he and her mother had done and that it was not fair because she was just a child and didn't deserve any of the fall-out resulting from her parents' indiscretion.

My son Mick said, "I will meet Claudia over my dead body. What do I want to meet her for?"

We knew it had nothing to do with the child and that in a way she was getting punished for what her father and mother did.

Apparently, Trevor had treated Jean badly as well and must have made her all sorts of promises about leaving me and going to her, promises that he knew he had no intentions of keeping.

Instead, the convenient thing was to have a nervous breakdown – that way he didn't have to take any responsibility, did he? He got ill with that nervous breakdown so things turned around.

That was my shame but he was the one who ended up having the nervous breakdown and having everyone running behind him and sending him to Switzerland to recover.

Why did I stay with him? I ask myself that question all the time. At one stage, I really despised him and later on that changed and I mellowed, but it took so long before I could make peace with what had happened. At least I didn't hate him as much as I did at the beginning.

If I am honest, I didn't want to leave our house and I think that is what kept me there more than anything else. Up to that point I had spent 43 years in our house. I had been there almost all my life in this country and it felt such a part of me.

It was a big decision and I usually have to have a lot of things against me before I decide to do something about a problem when it comes to making a life-changing decision. I think that's because I can shut off things and make out as if it never happened. Once I shut something off, it's off. Although I don't forget, I suppose I just bury it. I tend to shut something off and move on.

Trevor had been careless. You know how many letters he'd put down in the house that I had read? I'm talking about personal letters, some of which were for or from his mistress. He didn't put them down for me to find, but I found them and read them. So, I suppose it was really only a matter of time before he was caught out by his own carelessness.

Does that mean that I had suspected something? I honestly can't say that I had. I suppose I took a lot of things for granted and ignored what I chose to ignore.

As for Jean, she probably didn't think she had done anything wrong because if he was coming there every night and I seemed to be encouraging him, then what were they to do? I naively thought they were working on a book, not a baby.

Besides, I didn't know what he was telling her, so maybe he had spun her a line that we were married in name only, or some shit like that. You know, those classic words: "My wife doesn't understand me" that some foolish women will fall for when they have an affair with a married man.

But I was surprised that nobody said anything to me. All those friends and family members who knew but no-one had the courage to tell me. Nobody in my industry seemed to know anything about it because I'm a very private person, not a showbiz person, so most of my private life was very much out of the spotlight. There wasn't any big exposé in the *News of the World* or anything sordid like that.

Even now, when I say anything to showbiz people about Trevor's affair, they're surprised and didn't know anything about that unfortunate episode.

In 1995, we spent Christmas with his family in Trinidad and while we were there his mother started going a bit senile and I told him that she was going senile but he wouldn't accept it and kept saying she was just a bit forgetful.

His father had died in 1994 and I don't think he could countenance the idea of his mother becoming ill, even though she was 85. His world seemed to be caving in on him.

In 1995 he was officially retired from work and that was unexpected. He hadn't made any plans for it and was suddenly lost and feeling worthless.

I suppose those who wanted to apply for work could do so but Trevor just accepted the redundancy. And, you know it broke his heart when that happened because he never really applied for anything else.

I think it was the case that if you were applying for other work you would lose the full severance package, which he opted for. He thought he could take the redundancy payment and his time would be his own. And, as it was some time before the official retirement age, then he could do some consultancy work.

It was mainly the younger ones who applied for other jobs, anyway. At that time he also thought he was going to write something else, another book, but he never did.

He had always drunk alcohol but with all this stress he just plummeted and began to drink without any discretion. Although his drinking was never a secret, with all that was happening he just sank into a state where he drank morning, noon and night.

It was like he was losing his mind. From early in the morning he'd get up and go out the road to buy strong beers and lagers and come back home to drink them.

On top of that, he was drinking whatever else he could find around the house: bottles of wine or spirits that we had for guests. Then he'd go to bed and at about two o'clock in the morning – I called it the 'witching hour'– he'd get up and come and wake me up to ask for money to go and buy more booze.

We slept in separate rooms and every night he would creep into my room to pester me for money. He wouldn't buy alcohol and put it down in the house, he'd get up in the night to buy the strongest drinks he could find and then get off his head like those old soaks you see on park benches. The only difference was he was doing it in the house.

One day he just collapsed and we took him to the hospital and that's when they realised that his cholesterol was extraordinarily high. By that time he also found out that he had a prostrate problem and high blood pressure as well. He had all these things wrong with him but he was still drinking.

Things went from bad to worse. The doctors advised him to go and see a psychiatrist and, at one time while Lorna and I were in Trinidad, they hospitalised him because he'd drunk so much that he became paralytic.

His blood alcohol was so high that they kept him in, and subsequently, whenever he drank so much and got into trouble he would go up there and admit himself and then discharge himself when he was ready. He would treat it like a pop-in or day centre.

Marie, his psychiatrist, was so nice and she became a good friend of mine. Yet, Trevor was always so quick to say sorry afterwards and then he felt that as long as he had said sorry for any bad behaviour, which was the end of it. But, although it was the end for him it was not for me and he couldn't understand that. It really got out of hand.

One day, Trevor and I were having a discussion and talking good-good as though nothing awful had ever happened between us, then I went upstairs. He came up a while afterwards and said, matter-of-factly, "Guess what? I just told your sister that I'm going to kill you."

And with that he went out, closed the door and went back downstairs.

I took that threat seriously and put a lock on the door after that. I phoned up Marie, the psychiatrist, who wasn't there so I left a message on her answer phone saying, "Trevor's just told me he's going to kill me, what do I do? If you get this message, please call me as soon as possible."

When she got the message she called the house and Trevor took the call. She started talking to him as though nothing had happened and didn't mention anything about my call.

Then he said to her, "I just told Lorna that I'm going to kill Corinne."

Marie said, "Where is Corinne, is she in the house?"

He said, "Yes".

So she calmly asked to speak to me and he called to me, "Corinne, pick up the phone, Marie wants to talk to you."

She came on the phone and asked me if I have somewhere to go and I told her yes, so she said, "Get some things together. I'm coming to see him."

Then I went upstairs to Lorna's room and said to her, "Didn't Trevor tell you that he was going to kill me?"

Lorna said, "Yes, but I didn't pay any attention to him – he's just a drunken fool. I ain't bothered with him."

So, I said, "Marie is bothered with him and she's taking it seriously."

I quietly phoned Dian-Marie, my daughter, and told her to come for me and while I was waiting for her he started shouting for me to come down to him. That decided it. I made up my mind to get out of there fast and I just went downstairs and left the house right away.

Marie wasn't supposed to make home visits but she came to the house the next day for a meeting, which I attended. Trevor didn't turn up. The clinic was going to remove him from the house that day and at that time they told me that they could have sectioned him under the Mental Health Act and get the police to remove him from the house.

I didn't want to do that because I didn't think that he needed that level of control. I didn't think he was mad I just thought he was uncontrollably drunk, although that level of drunkenness is surely a type of madness.

All he had to say about the threat to kill me was, "Corinne, you can't take a joke."

And that's how Lorna had treated it as well. She didn't take it seriously but the hospital took it seriously and so did I, that's why I left the house. And I must say that when he made that threat to me I armed myself with a knife and if he'd come anywhere near me he'd have been killed because I was determined to use it. It was a good thing that I left the house before anything like that happened, because you never know.

They didn't section him and Marie made another appointment to come and see him at the house and she spoke to him. He was reasonable although he collapsed and we had to call an ambulance to get him to the hospital. They examined him and found that he was dehydrated.

That was the pattern of things. I remember one time I had to call the police to help me because of something he did and they came and wanted to take him away but I had to insist it wasn't so serious. He hadn't assaulted me or anything although I can't remember why I had called them. But ever since that day he would remind me, "And you called the police on me!"

Often, he would go up to the detox unit at the hospital, admit himself, have fun in there, take charge of the other patients, sort out their problems and then when he was ready he would discharge himself and come home.

While he was up there he wasn't dealing with his own problems, he was taking charge and running his own little kingdom because these people latched on to him and looked up to him.

That's why I say he had an inferiority complex because he wouldn't deal with himself and his inadequacies he wanted to run the world while drinking himself into a stupor. The drink would hide away his failings and short comings, or so he thought.

Eventually, I left him. It was 2004 and I went to spend three months in Trinidad. He kept phoning up and crying, "You go and leave me!"

And he did nothing in the house, so the place was in a state and he was in a state, as I discovered when I returned from my holiday.

On one visit to the house I went to use the toilet and it was filthy. That was the March. I moved back in temporarily to help him sort himself and the place out.

On the first night when I returned I went to bed and he jumped in the bed with me which I hadn't expected. I told him to get lost, I didn't want to sleep with him, so he came round the other side of the bed and grabbed my hand.

In a sudden flash I knew I wasn't going to stay there any longer. I stopped struggling with him long enough for him to ease his grip, then I grabbed my clothes and dashed down the stairs. He tried to chase me but he fell because he was drunk which gave me enough time to run down the stairs.

This was three o'clock in the morning and I ran for my life, grabbed my coat, quickly unlocked the door and dashed out of the house. He tried to chase me again but I was too quick. I ran to a neighbour and she opened the door and phoned Dian-Marie and Mick.

I was wearing my night clothes with an overcoat when Dian-Marie came to get me. I went to stay with her. Some time later I did go to try and arrange a meeting between Trevor and the doctor, which I also attended. He came to the meeting and started carrying on about how everyone was 'ganging up' on him and how everyone was 'on my side'.

He told the doctor, "I didn't do anything wrong, I only made a joke with her that I was going to kill her. The trouble is she can't take a joke."

He couldn't see that he was spiralling out of control. One of the problems with Trevor was that he had an extremely bad temper which he kept under control somehow. Unfortunately, around this time he was building up to a bad temper with me and I was scared because I didn't know how far he would go if he suddenly snapped.

As far as I was concerned there was nothing funny about his so-called 'joke' about killing me. Do I think he was capable of it? Judging by his fierce temper I would be inclined to say 'yes'. The fact that those words could even come from his lips spoke volumes about his unpredictability. Under the influence of alcohol, who knows what could have happened?

I remember when we were younger, not long after I had come to this country, we were at Victoria train station in London, which is very busy station; always crowded with commuters at the best of times. Someone hurried past us and jostled me.

In a flash, Trevor jumped in and was very aggressive towards that man. I could see that if he had come any closer or touched me again, Trevor could have attacked him. I would go as far as to say I think he could have killed him, he was that angry.

His face was like thunder. I remember being shocked and embarrassed but afterwards he calmed down and I suppose like everything else that I find disturbing I just put it out of my mind.

However, as he got older, Trevor's ferocious temper was becoming more and more unpredictable and uncontrollable. The other thing that bothered me even more than the rage was the fact that he never remembered anything after the event because he would have blackouts and he suffered from memory loss.

That is the part that really shocked and scared me: the fact that he could do and say the most terrible things but the next day he would not remember a thing about it.

It was only after Lorna died that I found I had to face a lot of things that I had postponed, like leaving that man.

When she died I used to tell him, "Lorna's gone now and she was the buffer between us."

Trevor was always very jealous of Lorna because I did everything with her and when she died he thought he had me to himself at last, but he was wrong.

After I left him, Trevor never gave up chasing me and trying to get us back together, but he thought I was one of his possessions. He acted as though he owned me and he could have no peace until he had me back in his grip. It was never in my head to go back but he never gave up.

I have lived a split existence my whole life. When I left Trevor I never wondered about him or worried about him; I just separated myself. I left that part of my life when I moved out.

The one regret that I had was that he died alone in the house in 2008. No-one was there with him except his beloved dog, Jebb, which was cowering in a corner when Mick arrived home and made the shocking discovery that Trevor had died.

It was sad and shocking for all of us but, because this man was someone who had been part of my life since we were children, it was an especially tragic and chilling episode for me.

Before she died some years before this, Lorna had always been worried about dying on her own and she begged us not to leave her alone. So, when she was ill in the hospital, she had me sleeping there every night for a month until she passed away.

That is the one thing I do regret with Trevor, the manner of his death. I felt bad and somewhat guilty that he had died on his own, just as his famous cousin, Claudia Jones, had died a lonely death all those years ago in the 1960s.

That kind of lonely death is something I don't think should happen to anyone. But even today there is an unbreakable bond between Lorna and myself. She is the first thing that comes into my thoughts when I wake up in the morning and the last thing I think about every night.

Chapter Eighteen

Keeping the Faith

In times of thanksgiving, disappointment, sadness, sickness, death, or even infidelity, the church has always played a big part in my life. I am High Church Anglican, and am almost tunnel-visioned about my religion.

I was baptised and confirmed in St Crispin's Church in Trinidad, which is High Church, and I have never taken to Anglican churches that are not High Church (in other words, English Catholic churches).

When I go back to Trinidad, if I can't get to my church of choice, I make do and go to the Roman Catholic church which, over there, is like High Church Anglican. Some people say that we High Church Anglicans are more Catholic than the Catholics!

I am a creature of habit. My cousin Lorna and I used to go to a foreign country every Easter so that we could spend the Easter weekend going to a Catholic church. I would never go to another country and go into the Anglican church there, I'd go to the Catholic church because I understand what's going on. I don't need to have a hymn book or prayer book because I know the liturgy. The only thing I don't know is the lesson which, of course, the priest will deliver.

Once, we went to Lourdes in France, the site of the famous shrine, and we visited religious sites in Spain, Portugal, Italy and other parts of Europe. I still like spending Easter in different countries so that I can go to a Roman Catholic church. The Catholics really go overboard at Easter, and I like to go to Rome during that time because it's fantastic. Everyone gets caught up in the religious atmosphere.

I was born into that ritual and as a child I went to church every Sunday morning. We were pristine in our frilly clothes, bobby socks and ribbons. Whether you believed or didn't believe in God, you went to church. Afterwards, we children went home for lunch then went back to Sunday school. That was the routine.

Some of my family were Seventh Day Adventists , so a lot of the time we went to that church as well. It didn't really matter, as long as we were seen to be going to church. Consequently, religion, and, more precisely, church-going, has always been a big thing in our family.

When I left Trinidad and came to England I had letters from my church introducing me to the church over here. In those days, church doors were left open all day, so people could go in and pray or seek spiritual guidance. It doesn't happen like that any more. For a start, it's not safe.

And then, somewhere along the line, I stopped going to church regularly, although I used to go on and off from time to time, but I never stopped saying my prayers at home. My beliefs were always there, which means I always found the time to say my prayers, morning and evening.

In spite of my own religious persuasion, I have an issue with other people trying to push their religion down my throat. I have a short temper with that and can be very rude if anyone tries to force their religion on me by telling me what I should or shouldn't believe. I don't go preaching my religion to anybody and I don't want anybody preaching theirs to me, either.

At one time, my cousin Lorna and I used to leave home and drive to Westminster Abbey on Sunday mornings. She would go to the Cathedral, because she was Catholic, and I would go to the Abbey because I am High Church Anglican. So we used to do that and then meet up afterwards, have lunch, do whatever we wanted to do in central London and then go back home. That was our recipe for the perfect Sunday.

As a boy, Trevor was also christened and confirmed in the same church as me. When he travelled to England he never bothered about church any more and stopped going. Most communists don't believe in God but he never lost his faith, he just put church-going on the back burner. Eventually, years after he'd retired he started going back to church and attended the same church as me.

I started going back to church every day and I think that was almost certainly because of Trevor's affair, when he went and strayed. At first I didn't speak to anybody in the church about what had happened, but just being there was consolation enough.

I was experiencing a lot of hurt, anger and bitterness, that goes without saying. I felt anything but forgiveness towards the man who had betrayed and humiliated me and our family, but somehow I had a great deal of peace whenever I went to church. I think that played a big part in bringing about the healing that I so desperately needed.

So, yes, while some people might consider it as escapism, or whatever they want to call it, for me going to church was comforting. I didn't go for counselling or anything to begin with, I just counselled myself and left God to do the rest.

When I'm angry or upset I discard those feelings and shut them away, but I keep thinking that whatever has happened to me, someone, somewhere, has it worse.

That's my philosophy in life. I hear people say, "Why me?", but I just say, "Why not me?" If I hope for something and it doesn't happen, I say, "Well, it wasn't supposed to happen."

I think that summarises my whole attitude and philosophy towards life.

After Lorna died I kept on going to my church and found the peace and comfort more beneficial than ever.

After I left Trevor, I attended church for some time before I started getting counselling. By then he was also being counselled but I decided to ask the priest to give us some sort of counselling together so we went for a couple of sessions there. The priest had experience as a psychologist and trained counsellor so that was useful.

Trevor's motivation was that he wanted me to go back to him but I knew that wouldn't work. We were counselled together and separately but as long as Trevor wasn't getting his own way he would come to the conclusion that "everybody was taking Corinne's side".

He was a selfish person in a lot of ways; everything had to be his way or it was the highway. If he was at a conference, he would talk and talk and never finish to let others have a chance to speak. He would always say, "Hold on, I haven't finished yet."

At home, he did the same thing and that would be the killer for me. I would cut off the conversation straight away but he always had to have the floor otherwise he would sulk.

Never mind the *Incredible Hulk*, on such occasions Trevor was the Incredible Sulk.

Chapter Nineteen

Glad to be a Gooner

I have always been sports minded. As a child in Trinidad I played all different sports: netball, cricket, athletics, tennis — in fact everything that young people did. We used to have inter-collegiate competitions which I always used to attend as a member of a team. And, because I was so sporty, I belonged to an athletics club called Bara-juan which used to compete in a range of different activities.

I was also always interested in football. We had a local football club called Essex that modelled itself on the English football teams, and we would get news of what was happening in the English game and support whichever team took our fancy.

When I came to England and settled in North London, Arsenal became my club, and that is how it has remained. I used to go to watch football, especially Arsenal home matches. I also went to watch cricket at the Oval and Lord's.

That's another game that we supported in Trinidad as well, and in those days it was the national game. As children we used to have half days from school and when cricket was on we went to watch it. So, I grew up participating in or watching sports and that is something that continued in my adult life, at least the watching if not the doing.

In London as it turned out, the Arsenal club was very near to our house and it was easy to go and see their home games. At first I went by myself and later the children got involved.

Dian-Marie inherited my love of sports and she was very athletic. Pretty soon, she joined me on the terraces at the Arsenal matches and even took up playing basketball and soccer, although Mick didn't go to football a lot he was more interested in basketball and played professionally, winning a whole lot of trophies. He is still involved in the game as a coach and referee.

So, we went to watch Arsenal which became our favourite team. It was just on our doorstep and we showed our loyalty to our local side and, in time, being an Arsenal supporter became a bit like being part of a family because the club always gave the impression of being a community team.

In the early days when we started supporting Arsenal, the two main north London sides were Arsenal and Tottenham Hotspur. The two of them were terrible rivals and sworn enemies. That's no understatement because the enmity between them runs so deep that I think blood has been shed over the years.

There was quite a bit of racism in football in the sixties and seventies, but we found that the Arsenal side was more tolerant and the supporters were not as racist as some other teams.

Some of the teachers who taught at Trevor's school were scouts for Tottenham but Trevor said they discouraged him from putting forward any of the black boys from the school to be scouted for the Tottenham team.

That was terrible, because there were some fine athletic boys at the school and they might have made it as first-class footballers. Thankfully, things are different now. All the clubs have black players and there is nothing unusual about that.

At one point in the old days, Arsenal was more of an Irish team because there was a large Irish population in the area, but now the team is made up of players and supporters from just about everywhere, what matters is the talent.

One thing we can say about our side is that we are nurturing the young English players in the academy. If we don't support the young up-coming footballers then the English game will be full of foreign players and those born in England won't get a look-in, so I think it's good that the young ones are being trained at the highest level to take the team forward in the future.

I think it was a stroke of genius when the Arsenal Manager, Arsene Wenger, brought the young player Theo Walcott into the squad. He was just a teenager of 16 and some of the other big clubs were trying to sign him up as well.

When Arsenal got him we were really excited because he was fast and showed a lot of potential. He really captured the imagination of the then England manager, Sven Jorgen-Erickson, who included Walcott in England's World Cup squad. Arsenal has a lot of women supporters and I am proud to be a committed fan with my own season ticket. Judging from the matches I see on television, I think arsenal has more women supporters than any of the other team.

We're very loyal and we're just as vocal as the men, believe me, except you won't hear many women swearing. The rules are marked up in our impressive, multi-million pound stadium, The Emirates: 'no swearing, no racist remarks...', and so on. You find most people are respectful because our team is not known for hooliganism.

When it comes to travelling to away games or supporting the team come rain or shine, we're up there with the best of them. We have just grown with the club. You hear people saying, "I've been with this club over 40 years, or 50 years". They are very staunch supporters and for some people it's almost like a religion.

Trevor liked football up to a point and went with us to a couple of matches but he was never as fanatical about the game as I was.

Arsenal supporters are called Gooners, and I am proud to have that title. I get a kick out of calling myself a Gooner.

It was really exciting when I found out that people like the American film director Spike Lee was also a Gooner and would turn up at matches wearing the team colours and his famous baseball cap.

We really had our heyday when Arsene Wenger took over as manager and there were players in the squad like Thierry Henry and Patrick Viera, truly first-class players who had an international fan base. Other teams envied our club and many people who weren't even football fans took to us because of the handsome, talented players in our team.

Those players gave the squad what Henry called the 'Va-va voom!' Those were the famous words he used in a TV commercial to advertise a car. That commercial really raised his profile as well, and, because he was such a good player and a cool, good-looking guy, a lot of younger people and especially women supporters began to take an interest in Arsenal Football Club.

I am so fanatical about my team and my football that I am sure some people will think I am out of my mind, especially when I go on and on about the squad. I am a big talker anyway, but when it comes to Arsenal, I can talk until the cows come home.

I go on and on about it so much and never get tired. In fact, I have even taken to calling up the office and letting them have a piece of my mind when they do stupid things that may have cost us a match.

I will tell you that I never miss a home game and the way I feel so passionate about it, I am sure I would be an asset to the team if I was on the bench as one of Arsene Wenger's advisers or coaches.

Sometimes those boys just need slapping into shape and, unfortunately, Arsene is so biased that he never admits that our boys are capable of making errors. He always finds excuses and blames the other side or something or the other to explain why we performed badly or got slaughtered when we should have put in a better performance.

For me, football really is the 'beautiful game' and no team plays it with as much style and passion as Arsenal. That's why I am proud to be a fan and will be a Gooner till I die.

Chapter Twenty

Endings and Beginnings

When my cousin Lorna died I was absolutely devastated and totally grief-stricken. On the very day that we buried her, Egbert, another one of my cousins, also died.

As I have said before, Lorna was practically my sister; the two of us had grown up together and we were virtually identical, especially in the way we looked.

People were always getting us mixed up and we enjoyed that, especially because there was always the scope for making mischief if we felt like it.

Although we knew she was ill and wouldn't recover, when she eventually died her loss was almost unbearable. On top of that, Egbert's passing so soon afterwards became the straw that broke the camel's back.

Around that time — poignantly it was close to Easter — I had started rehearsing for a play, but this particular weekend I got up and was very emotional.

As much as I say that I don't get emotional, I woke up one morning and was crying and carrying on in a most peculiar way. I told everyone that I couldn't do the play because I had too much on my head.

My daughter, Dian-Marie and her aunt Myrna, were very concerned. Their solution was to take me shopping.

Usually, whenever I'm stressed or feeling a bit down, I go for walks to clear my head, but this time the pair of them took me off for a little retail therapy and we shopped all day and came back home feeling a bit more relaxed.

I still felt I couldn't do the play, though, so I rang the agent and left a message and then rang the director. Unfortunately, the publicity had already gone out saying Corinne Skinner Carter from *Eastenders* would be appearing in the production.

There was no understudy and we still had about a week-and-a-half rehearsal time, but I felt I couldn't do it. That Tuesday morning they called and said they understood that I had reservations about doing the play because they knew I was under a lot of pressure.

In the end I didn't do the play and when all the dust had settled I told myself that I had to do a play, a big part, and that would be the last production I was going to do.

Almost as soon as I had that conversation with myself, I got a play, *Prospects*, at the Soho Theatre.

Everyone in the production found it a difficult play to do. Every night was difficult and I've never prayed so much in my life. I prayed that everything would be all right and that I wouldn't forget my lines. I even prayed that time would hurry up and the production would end.

In the end, we completed the run and the play came to an end and got good reviews. At the after party that night I told them all that that was my last big part, I would only be doing cameos from then on.

Everyone said to me, "Don't be silly, Corinne."

But I insisted, "That is it, I'm not doing anything like that again."

And I will not. I will not put myself through that torture again.

Some time afterwards I went to an audition for one of Allistair Bain's plays and I had to ring him up and tell him that I didn't know whether I was being offered the part but I didn't want it because I didn't think I could do it. And he understood, so, that was that.

Looking back over my career, I would say that the production I most enjoyed doing was the film *Dreaming Rivers (1988)*, which I did for Sankofa Films.

That film took me to Martinique when they had their first Caribbean Film Festival.

The film was directed by Martina Attille and was such a beautifully simple story, and a lovely production to work on.

We started working on the film in 1987 and it so happened that on one of the days that we were supposed to have been filming a big storm happened in England that blew down all the trees and brought the whole country to a standstill. That was the famous hurricane that none of the weather forecasters saw coming.

I think it was a woman, an amateur meteorologist, who had called the BBC that night to say that she feared a big storm was coming. The weather announcer broadcast on air that the woman had made the call but he told her, rather patronisingly, that no such thing was going to happen. Famous last words!

That night, all hell broke loose and Britain was lashed by the fiercest storms possibly in its whole history. The storm struck overnight and, oh my gosh, what a night and day that was: nobody could leave their homes the next morning.

I mean, people couldn't go to work, kids couldn't get to school, buses and other transport were down, and there were power cuts, trees, power lines and roofs were blown down and littered the streets.

It was a proper hurricane just like the type we get in the Caribbean. A hurricane in England! Would you believe it?

The UK had never seen anything like it. I remember it so well and automatically associate it with the film because it put a temporary stop to the production, at least on one of the days we were supposed to have been shooting.

Dreaming Rivers was a bitter-sweet, emotional story about my character, an elderly Caribbean woman called Miss T, whose story is played out as she reflects on her life from her death bed.

A child is sitting by the side of the bed and Miss T is reminiscing about all the things that happened to her over the course of her life.

She's all alone as her husband has gone and so have all the children, who have grown up and flown the nest. But the film was not just about her life, it was also about the lives of black people as immigrants in Britain, and had a sense of two homes: here and the countries they had come from.

You know, I am still so struck by the story and the way it was produced, the whole atmosphere, the storyline, the screenplay, the costumes; everything about it was fantastic.

I thought it was a sensitive and thoughtful story, and it was unusual to have had the opportunity to do something so beautiful and thought-provoking. It was a very rare production and even today we don't really see such issues portrayed in film, which is a great shame.

Martina was such a good director and the crew around her was fantastic. We were given such a good reception in Martinique and it was so refreshing to be in such a creative environment surrounded by film people from all over the world.

Aside from taking us to the film festival in Martinique, one of the first black international film festivals, the film also went to France and a number of other places to various other film competitions. Over the years, it has been shown all over the world.

The film *Burning an Illusion (1981)*, directed by Menelik Shabazz, was also screened in Martinique at the film festival that year. I had a part in that as well, and it so happened that I was also in a third film that was shown at the festival: *Pressure (1975)*, directed by Horace Ové. So, I was in three films at a landmark film festival and feeling on top of the world.

Burning an Illusion told the story of Pat, a bright young black woman, played by Cassie McFarlane, and her relationship with Del, played by Victor Romero-Evans. The film was about this young woman's dreams of a 'happy ever after' relationship, which turns sour when her boyfriend moves in with her.

Instead of pulling his weight, he takes her for granted and on top of that loses his job, which creates tensions between them. They also face a lot of social pressures which impacts on their relationship.

I played Pat's mother. Let's face it, I was almost always playing someone's mother by then. But the film was given such a good reception: really good reviews, and Cassie even won an *Evening Standard* film award in 1982.

It was a good experience to be part of that scene because Menelik and a few others were making such bold films to tell black people's stories, warts and all, in a way that hadn't been done before.

You have to remember that there was nothing on the big screen coming out of Britain that was being made by blacks, for blacks.

Horace's film, *Pressure*, was probably the first off the mark and was probably the first black feature film made in this country.

It was gritty and in-your-face because it dared to show the social pressures black people were facing which made some of them turn radical in order to make sense of their lives and try to find a way of coping with racism.

Pressure told the story of a young man who had recently left school and, although he was top of his class and got lots of qualifications, he couldn't get a job. While he was 'very English' and ordinary, his older brother, played by Horace James, was very much into the Black Power Movement, although his family disapproved.

The film really showed the problem of how black people were facing discrimination by the police and ignorant whites in the society.

I played an auntie in that film and had to try and get the distracted lead character back on the straight and narrow by taking him to church, where Norman Beaton was terrific as the Pentecostal church minister.

People often commented that Norman and I were the two main faces they remembered seeing on television back then. We worked together on a lot of productions, mainly on television but also in films like *Pressure*. We were all learning, really.

It was a big transition to go from dancing to doing plays, to television and then film, but it all felt perfectly natural to me. It didn't really matter what the medium was, I was just excited to be doing work that I enjoyed with people who enjoyed it as much as I did.

Among the people that were in show business when I came to this country were outstanding performers like Nadia Catouse, Cy Grant, Earl Cameron and Edric Connor — all of whom I admired and had the opportunity to work with.

The pool of black actors back then was relatively small, so when you think about it, it was probably inevitable that we would all end up working together on one project or another.

Ram John Holder, who's from Guyana, is someone else who has had a long career and is probably best known for starring with Norman Beaton in the TV show *Desmond's*.

Anyway, he and I have appeared together in a number of things, including a film called, *The Future's Getting Old Like the Rest of Us (2010)*, which was commissioned by the Serpentine Gallery. That was a really interesting and challenging production to do.

It was set in an old people's home and featured eight characters named by letters, from A to H. I played character B. It was quite experimental in many ways and one of the things about it was that we were all required to deliver our lines simultaneously. If you can imagine eight voices all speaking at the same time, then you'll get the idea.

The script was based on real life stories or experiences and was written vertically, not horizontally. It was quite a difficult part to do and at first I didn't want to do it. Then, they came up with the idea of giving me an earpiece and re-writing the character as being deaf. That way, they could feed me my lines, which was great.

It turned out that in the end I wasn't the only one of the actors using an earpiece; several of the other characters also needed the device.

Looking back over my life has been really interesting and has given me a lot to think about. I started out in the 1950s with the dancing, then packed that in and took up acting.

And the more I think about it, I'm one of a few black performers left in the industry from those days. I'm also one of the very few who had the opportunity to do a variety of things, crossing the boundaries between TV, film and the stage.

I had the chance to perform in a number of things, some of which, like *Empire Road*, pushed the boundaries and made history. And, of course, there was the teaching, which I am especially proud of.

My family's attitude towards my showbiz career is similar to my own: it's neither here nor there. If my family is proud and amazed at my achievements, they've never told me. I think as far as they're concerned, it's just normal for me to be doing what I do. Those are the only words I can think of using because we're all expected to fulfill our dreams and ambitions.

A few years ago, Leo, one of my brothers who lived in Trinidad, was shocked at the amount of things I had done over the course of my life.

He said, "Corinne, you come down here on holiday and you're so quiet about what you're up to in England. You never say anything about what you're doing. If we're lucky we get to hear from other people."

In the family home, where I used to live before I left for England, they have put up pictures of me from various shows I've been in. But for all that the attitude is still very low key.

I remember in 2007 my father's family had a big reunion. It was a massive gathering with hundreds of people from all over the world, including a certain amount of folks I had never met. My closest cousin, Myrna, always talks about me and she decided to do a presentation highlighting my life and achievements.

Everyone was amazed and had no idea that I was so accomplished. It transpired that another one of my cousins holds a doctorate and works at the University of the West Indies where she immediately set up an archive for my work.

So, at least that has happened in my lifetime and I have been able to see it and get an idea of how much pleasure my work has given people over the years. To me, that is the best tribute of all, knowing that my work has been appreciated.

My career was quite accidental in the first place: I didn't set out with the idea that I was going to be a dancer and actress. All I knew for sure was that I wanted to be a teacher. In the end, I did all three and that's the icing on the cake.

The way I see it, my showbiz career found me. How else could I explain how an ordinary girl like me from Trinidad made it up there on the big screen, on TV and on stage?

Talent, luck and opportunity have all played their part in my life and career and I am so blessed to know that in an industry that is so cut-throat and fickle, somehow I managed to survive as long as I did.

You could say that time and time again, like a cat with nine lives, Corinne Skinner Carter managed to land on her feet.